SIX GREAT IDEAS

TRUTH · GOODNESS · BEAUTY
LIBERTY · EQUALITY · JUSTICE

MORTIMER J. ADLER

SIX GREAT IDEAS

TRUTH · GOODNESS · BEAUTY
Ideas We Judge By
LIBERTY · EQUALITY · JUSTICE
Ideas We Act On

COLLIER BOOKS
MACMILLAN PUBLISHING COMPANY
NEW YORK
COLLIER MACMILLAN PUBLISHERS
LONDON

To the benefactors and trustees
of the
Institute for Philosophical Research

Macmillan Publishing Company
866 Third Avenue, New York, N.Y. 10022
Collier Macmillan Canada, Inc.

Library of Congress Cataloging in Publication Data
Adler, Mortimer Jerome, 1902–
    Six great ideas.
    1. Truth. 2. Good and evil. 3. Aesthetics.
4. Liberty. 5. Equality. 6. Justice (Philosophy)
I. Title.
BD171.A24   1984   111'.8   83-18888
ISBN 0-02-072020-3 (pbk.)

First Collier Books Edition 1984

151413

Six Great Ideas is also published in a hardcover
edition by Macmillan Publishing Company.

Printed in the United States of America

Contents

Preface   ix

PART ONE. PROLOGUE: THE GREAT IDEAS

1 Philosophy's Business   3

2 Plato, Right *and* Wrong   7

3 The Vocabulary of Thought   13

4 These Chosen Few   20

PART TWO. IDEAS WE JUDGE BY: TRUTH, GOODNESS, AND BEAUTY

5 The Liar and the Skeptic   31

6 Milder Forms of Skepticism   39

7 The Realm of Doubt   46

8 The Pursuit of Truth   56

9 From Truth to Goodness and Beauty   64

10 Is and Ought   66

11 Real and Apparent Goods   72

12 The Range and Scale of Goods   82

13 The Ultimate and Common Good   92

14 From Truth and Goodness to Beauty   99

15 Enjoyable Beauty   103

16 Admirable Beauty   111

17 The Goodness of Beauty and the Beauty of Truth   123

PART THREE. IDEAS WE ACT ON: LIBERTY, EQUALITY, AND JUSTICE

18 The Sovereignty of Justice   135

19 The Freedom to Do as One Pleases   140

20 The Liberties to Which We Are Entitled   149

21 The Dimensions of Equality   155

22 The Equalities to Which We Are Entitled   164

23 The Inequalities That Justice Also Requires   174

24 The Domain of Justice   186

25 The Justice and the Authority of Law   197

PART FOUR. EPILOGUE: GREAT ISSUES AND QUESTIONS

26 Ideas, Issues, and Questions   209

27 Concerning Truth, Goodness, and Beauty   212

28 Concerning Liberty, Equality, and Justice   228

Preface

IT IS WITH THE KIND OF PIETY that Confucius thought should be accorded our ancestors for their contribution to our being that I look upon the sources of this book. I am also observing the Mosaic precept to honor one's father and mother, understood in the broadest sense as paying homage to the sources of one's understanding as well as of one's being.

Working for the Encyclopaedia Britannica Company and with Robert Hutchins at the University of Chicago in editing and publishing *Great Books of the Western World*, I produced two volumes on the great ideas, entitled the *Syntopicon*. These were intended to guide readers to the important passages in which the discussion of the great ideas can be found in the great books. In the course of that work, I wrote essays on each of the 102 great ideas, which comprise the chapters of the *Syntopicon*.

The first exploration of the whole realm of great ideas, each in itself and in relation to others, led naturally and almost inevitably to the inception of the Institute for Philosophical Research, conceived as a group of scholars dedicated to cooperative work on the great ideas. Their objective was to take stock of what had been thought about each of those ideas in the whole tradition of Western thought, to identify the diversity of meanings that constitute their inner complexity, to formulate the questions about them that had been disputed, and to examine as well as to assess the opposed voices in the controversies that ensued.

The Institute for Philosophical Research was established in 1952 by a grant from the Ford Foundation when Paul Hoffman and Robert Hutchins were, respectively, its president and vice-president, and by a grant from the Old Dominion Foundation. Since 1956, it has enjoyed sustained and sustaining support from Paul Mellon and Arthur A. Houghton, Jr.

In the course of almost thirty years it has made a good start on the enormous task to which it was originally dedicated. It could not in that time succeed in exploring the whole realm of the great ideas to an extent and to a depth that went far beyond the initial exploration of them in the *Syntopicon*. It would probably take five times thirty years, or even more, to complete the job that the Institute set for itself.

Nevertheless, the work it has accomplished since 1952 is a respectable and worthy beginning. Its senior fellows and their junior associates have engaged in research and collaboration and have done the writing that has resulted in the publication of a number of books or lengthy monographs: two volumes on the idea of freedom; one volume each on the ideas of justice, happiness, love, progress, and religion; and a monograph on the idea of beauty. With respect to the idea of equality, on which much work has been done over a period of years, a file of unpublished papers has been accumulated.

In addition, I must mention books that I have written during this period with the assistance of my colleagues at the Institute and subject to criticism and revision by them. Those that have a bearing on the six great ideas treated in this book include *The Conditions of Philosophy,* which dealt with the modes of truth and the distinction between knowledge and opinion in the realms of mathematics, science, history, and philosophy, as well as in the sphere of commonsense thought; *The Difference of Man and the Difference It Makes,* in which the equality in kind of all human beings was treated in the context of the difference in kind between man and lower animals; *The Time of Our Lives,* subtitled "The Common Sense of Ethics," in which the idea of the good and of man's ultimate good, which is happiness, received examination in the light of distinctions between real and apparent goods, needs and wants, natural and civil rights; *The Common Sense of Politics,* in which the sovereignty of justice was recognized as indispensable to reconciling liberty and equality and maximizing both harmoniously.

In the course of the last thirty years, I have also had the privilege and pleasure of moderating executive seminars conducted under the auspices of the Aspen Institute for Humanistic Studies. The program of readings in these seminars dealt with the ideas of liberty, equality, justice, rights, wealth and property, virtue and happiness. I have profited greatly from the discussions in which these seminars engaged, learning more, I suspect, about the great ideas being discussed than was learned by the participants who were being initiated into the consideration of them.

To all these sources of what is here written about six great ideas, I owe a debt of gratitude as well as an expression of homage and piety, most especially to the benefactors and trustees of the Institute for Philosophical Research, to whom this book is dedicated, as well as to all my many associates, past and present, at the Institute. I trust they will forgive me for not mentioning all their names.

Contrary to my usual habit, I have not appended a selected

bibliography at the end of this book. My reason is that readers who wish to consult the best texts on these great ideas can find them cited in the two volumes of the *Syntopicon* (in Chapters 6, 30, 42, 47, and 94), and also in the *Great Treasury of Western Thought*, in the production of which my Institute and Britannica colleague, Charles Van Doren, collaborated. There they will more easily find important passages on these great ideas, because there they are quoted in full, not merely cited as in the *Syntopicon* (see Chapter 6. Section 3; 9.6; 9.7; 12.2; 12.3; 13.2; 13.3; 16.6).

In closing this Preface, let me confess that I may be tempted in the years ahead to write another book about great ideas; but, with a book about the idea of God already published and with the publication of this one about six of the greatest ideas other than God, it may be that the next book will have to deal with some not so great ideas.

MORTIMER J. ADLER

Aspen, Colorado
July 1, 1980

PART ONE
Prologue: The Great Ideas

CHAPTER 1

Philosophy's Business

IT CANNOT BE TOO OFTEN REPEATED that philosophy is every-body's business. To be a human being is to be endowed with the proclivity to philosophize. To some degree we all engage in philosophical thought in the course of our daily lives.

Acknowledging this is not enough. It is also necessary to understand why this is so and what philosophy's business is.

The answer, in a word, is ideas. In two words, it is great ideas—the ideas basic and indispensable to understanding ourselves, our society, and the world in which we live.

These ideas, as we shall see presently, constitute the vocabulary of everyone's thought. Unlike the concepts of the special sciences, the words that name the great ideas are all of them words of ordinary, everyday speech. They are not technical terms. They do not belong to the private jargon of a specialized

[3]

branch of knowledge. Everyone uses them in ordinary conversation. But everyone does not understand them as well as they
can be understood, nor has everyone pondered sufficiently the
questions raised by each of the great ideas. To do that and to
think one's way through to some resolution of the conflicting
answers to these questions is to philosophize.

This book aims to do no more than to provide some guidance
in this process. Not for all of the great ideas; that would take a
very long book indeed. But for six of them, six of obvious importance to all of us: truth, goodness, and beauty on the one
hand; liberty, equality, and justice on the other.

I am not only limiting myself to the consideration of these six
ideas. I am also limiting the consideration of them to an elementary delineation of each idea that will try to achieve three
results for the reader.

First, it should give the reader a surer grasp of the various
meanings of the word he uses when he talks about the idea. In
the course of any week, every one of us probably says "That's
true" or "That's false" a dozen times. What do we mean when
we say that? By what criteria do we make that judgment? And
how can we support our judgment if the person we are talking
to challenges us? Getting the idea of truth a littler clearer than
it is for most people will help them to answer these questions.
When they move, even a little, toward a better understanding
of the idea of truth, they are, of course, philosophizing whether
or not they consciously think of themselves as doing so.

Second, the delineation of each idea should make the reader
more aware than he normally is of questions or issues that he
cannot avoid confronting if he is willing to think a little further
about the idea—basic ones, ones that human beings have been
arguing about over the centuries.

Does what is true change from time to time or is it immutable? Can one thing be true for me and the very opposite true
for you? Are all differences of opinion that divide persons into
opposing camps capable of being resolved by finding which of
the conflicting opinions is true and which false, or are some

differences of opinion not matters of truth and falsity at all? What is the answer to the skeptic who claims that the effort to get at the truth is always in vain?

Third, in the consideration of each idea, we are led to the consideration of other ideas. How does our understanding of truth affect our understanding of goodness and beauty? How does our understanding of what is good and bad carry us not only to an understanding of what is right and wrong, but also to an understanding of justice, and how does that affect our understanding of liberty and equality as well?

None of the great ideas is self-enclosed or sealed off from others. Hence, the delineation of each of the six ideas will carry us beyond that idea to one or more of the other five; and when we have considered all six, each in itself and each in relation to the others, we will find ourselves more at home in the whole realm of ideas, or at least more conversant with the bearing that these six ideas have on quite a large number of other great ideas. That is one reason why I have chosen these six. They are truly pivotal ideas—each a center around which a number of other great ideas revolve.

What I have just set down as things I hope to do for the reader is minimal. Much more than that can be done for each of the great ideas. I myself have written two large volumes on *The Idea of Freedom* and some of my colleagues at the Institute for Philosophical Research have written books about the idea of justice, the idea of love, the idea of happiness, the idea of progress, the idea of beauty, the idea of religion.

These books do a great deal more than what I plan to do here for the six ideas I have chosen. They attempt to take stock of all that has been written about a given idea in the whole tradition of Western thought and they try to clarify that discussion by identifying points of agreement and disagreement and assessing the arguments pro and con on all important issues. Consequently, they are full of quotations from the great thinkers of past and present and they are replete with footnotes. They are certainly worth studying, but they do need to be studied, not just read. In contrast, my plan for this book about six great ideas is to make it one that can be profitably read without being painstakingly studied.

I should also mention one other exploration of the world of the great ideas, in which I was engaged some forty years ago. Then, when the Encyclopaedia Britannica company decided to publish *Great Books of the Western World,* which I helped President Hutchins of the University of Chicago to edit, I prepared, as a guide to the discussion of the great ideas in the great books, something I called a *Syntopicon.* It was so called because it was a collection of some three thousand topics discussed in the great books, organized under each of 102 great ideas, together with references to passages in the great books topic by topic. For each of 102 outlines of topics, I wrote an essay setting forth the development of that idea in the tradition of Western thought, and indicating the major controversies that had emerged in that development.

The chapters in this book that deal with just six out of the 102 ideas about which I wrote essays in the *Syntopicon* will serve a different purpose. I shall not be concerned with the history of these ideas, though I will touch on some of the major controversies to which they have given rise. The *Syntopicon* essays were meant to serve as guides to reading what the most eminent authors in our Western civilization have thought about the great ideas. The chapters of this book are meant to help readers improve their own thinking about the six important subjects I have chosen.

If I succeed in that aim, I will have helped readers to engage in the business of philosophy, which is everybody's business not only because nobody can do much thinking, if any at all, without using the great ideas, but also because no special, technical competence of the kind that is required for the particular sciences and other specialized disciplines is required for thinking about the great ideas. Everybody does it, wittingly or unwittingly. I hope I am right in believing that everyone would wish to do it just a little better.

CHAPTER 2

Plato, Right **and** Wrong

WHEN ARISTOTLE'S NAME is turned into an adjective to modify a noun, it is usually attached to the word "logic." We say of an argument we have just listened to, "That's Aristotelian logic," sometimes intending to praise, sometimes to disparage.

So, when Plato's name is turned into an adjective, it is usually attached either to "love" or to "idea." We speak of a certain type of friendship as platonic love; or we say, "That's only a Platonic idea and it has nothing to do with reality."

What underlies the derogatory thrust of the phrase "Platonic idea" is, of course, Plato's theory of ideas, which is hardly a commonsense doctrine that most people readily embrace. On the contrary, when they understand it, they find it runs counter to their commonsense view of the way things are. But it is far

from being wholly wrong. Of the two central tenets of Plato's
theory of ideas, one was right and the other wrong.

Let us begin with what was wrong about it. For Plato, there
were two worlds, not one—the sensible world of changing
physical things that we apprehend by means of our senses and
the world of intelligible objects that we apprehend by means of
our intellects or minds. For him, both are real worlds, where
calling them "real" means that they exist independently of our
apprehending them.

Even if neither men nor other animals that have eyes or ears
or other senses existed, the world of sensible things would exist
exactly as it is. So, too, for Plato, even if there were no human
beings with the characteristic human ability to think of such
objects as truth and goodness, or justice and liberty, these objects would exist—exist independently of all thinking minds.
That is why in Plato's view, the idea of the good or the idea of
justice has a full measure of reality.

Plato went further. More than a full measure of reality, the
world of ideas had for him a superior grade of reality. The
physical things that we perceive through our senses come into
being and pass away and they are continually in flux, changing
in one way or another. They have no permanence. But though
we may change our minds about the ideas we think about, they
themselves are not subject to change. Unlike living organisms,
they are not born and do not die. Unlike stars and atoms, they
do not move about in space. Unlike the familiar physical objects
that surround us, they do not get hot or cold, larger or smaller,
and so on.

The world of changing physical things is thus for Plato a mere
shadow of the much more real world of ideas. When we pass
from the realm of sense experience to the realm of thought, we
ascend to a higher reality, for we have turned from things that
have no enduring existence to enduring and unchanging (Plato
would say "eternal") objects of thought—ideas.

For those of us who cannot shuck off our commitment to
common sense, Plato goes too far in attributing reality to ideas, .

and much too far in exalting their reality over the reality of sensible phenomena—the reality of the ever-changing world we experience through our senses. We do not hesitate to reject Plato's theory of ideas, and declare him wrong in attributing reality to ideas as well as to physical things, and a superior reality at that. For us commonsense fellows, it is the world of ideas that is comparatively shadowy as compared with the tangible, visible, audible world of things that press on us from all sides.

However, we, too, would be going too far if we regarded ideas as having no existence at all, or regarded them as existing only in our minds when we are thinking. That would make them entirely subjective, as subjective as the feeling of pain you experience when a finger is squeezed too hard, or as subjective as the toothache you have that you can tell me about but that I cannot experience because at the moment it is yours and yours alone.

Plato was right, not wrong, in holding that ideas are objects that the human mind can think about. He was right in insisting on their objectivity. This, understood in the simplest manner possible, amounts to saying that you and I can engage in conversation about one and the same idea because it is an object that you and I are thinking about, just as you and I can engage in conversation about one and the same overcoat when you help me put it on and ask me whether it is warm enough. When you and I discuss truth or justice, the idea of truth or justice is before our minds, or present to our minds, just as much as the overcoat that you help me on with is handled by both of us at the same time.

If anyone has difficulty in understanding this, it is because the word "idea" has two meanings, not one—one in which it is used to refer to something that is entirely subjective and one in which it is used to refer to something that is quite objective.

In the first meaning, the word has been used to refer to the whole range of entities that comprise the ideational content of our consciousness. In this broad sense of the word, it covers the sensations and perceptions we have, the images we form, the memories we summon up, and the conceptions or notions that we employ in our thinking.

When the word "idea" is used in this way by psychologists, all the various items referred to are certainly subjective. My sensations or perceptions are not yours; the images that occur in my dreams or the memories I dwell upon when I reminisce are mine alone; so, too, are the concepts or notions I have been at some pains to form as I study a difficult science.

To call them all "subjective" is simply to say that they are private, not public. When I speak of them as mine—my perception, my memory, or my concept—I am saying that the perception, memory, or concept in question belongs to me and me alone. You can have no access to it, just as you cannot have access to the toothache I am suffering.

In its other meaning, the word "idea" refers to an object that two or more persons can have access to, can focus on, can think about, can discuss. While this meaning may not be as familiar, neither is it entirely strange or puzzling.

If we disagree about a decision just handed down by the Supreme Court, we may find ourselves challenging each other's views about justice. If I ask you for your view of justice, I am asking you to tell me what you think about it, and I am also prepared to tell you what I think about it. The "it" here is justice as an object of thought, both your thought and mine, not justice as a concept in your mind, but not mine.

This is not to deny that you and I have concepts in our minds —concepts we think with when we think about justice. Furthermore, your concepts and mine are distinct. But that does not prevent both of us from thinking about one and the same object—an object of thought we call "justice," and sometimes refer to as "the idea of justice."

This runs parallel to saying that the quite distinct percepts you and I have are what enable us to perceive when we do perceive one and the same perceptible object. Even though I use my percept and you use yours, as means or instrumentalities for perceiving a sensible object, the sensible object that we both perceive (such as the overcoat you help me put on) remains one and the same. So, too, you have your memory and I have mine of a football game we both attended, but we can both remember one and the same forward pass that won a victory in the last minute of play.

Let me illustrate the point I am trying to make by harking back for a moment to the book I wrote about the idea of freedom. Because it attempted to examine the whole range of Western thought about freedom, it considered what has been written about that subject by hundreds of authors. Some of them by the way, used the word "freedom," and some used "liberty," but it was always perfectly clear that these were merely two words for the same object of thought.

However, it was not so clear that all of the authors who wrote about the subject, using either the word "freedom" or the word "liberty," were talking about one and the same object. Some, for example, concentrated wholly on the freedom persons enjoy when they can act as they please. This is the liberty of which a person in chains or in prison is deprived. Some were concerned with the freedom of the will—the freedom of choice that those who call themselves determinists deny.

The idea of freedom—or, what amounts to the same thing, freedom as an object of thought—includes both of the freedoms mentioned. When some authors write about freedom, they concentrate on one aspect of it, not another. But all the authors who concentrate on that one aspect of freedom are engaged in thinking about the same object. If that were not the case, it would be meaningless to say that they were in agreement or disagreement about it.

For example, thinking about freedom as consisting in being able to act as one pleases, certain authors hold it sufficient for such liberty to consist in exemption from physical coercion or duress. Others, disagreeing, hold that lack of enabling means might deprive a man of the liberty under consideration. For example, a person without sufficient money is not free to dine at the Ritz, if he or she wishes to.

There would be no disagreement here if both sets of authors

were not thinking and talking about one and the same object
—that aspect of freedom which consists in being able to act as
one wishes or do as one pleases.

What all this comes to can be summed up by advising readers
that this book about six great ideas is not concerned with psy-
chology. It is not concerned with what goes on in people's
minds when they think, or what concepts or notions they have
in their minds and employ to think with. It is concerned solely
with what they have before their minds when they engage in
thinking—with objects they are together considering and about
which they and other human beings over the centuries have
raised questions and, in answering them, have either agreed or
disagreed.

For anyone who is incurably addicted to the subjective sense
in which the word "idea" is used by most people, I would be
willing to drop the word entirely and substitute "object of
thought" for it. But I would much prefer retaining the word
and have my readers remember that, as I am using it in a book
about six great ideas, I am always writing about six great objects of thought that all of us can focus our minds on, not about
the particular concepts or notions that each of us may employ
in order to do that.

So far, then, Plato was right. Ideas, as objects of thought, do
exist. The idea of truth or of justice does not cease to exist when
I cease to think about it, for others can be thinking about it
when I am not. However, unlike the chair I am sitting on or the
book you are holding in your hand, which does not cease to
exist as a perceptible object when no one is perceiving it, objects of thought do cease to exist as intelligible objects when no
one at all is thinking about them.

There would be stars and atoms in the physical cosmos with
no human beings or other living organisms to perceive them.
But there would be no ideas as objects of thought without
minds to think about them. Ideas exist objectively, but not with
the reality that belongs to physical things. On that point, Plato
was wrong.

CHAPTER 3

The Vocabulary of Thought

"THAT'S JUST A PLATONIC IDEA and has nothing to do with reality." The slurring dismissal hurled by that statement against the consideration of ideas calls for a reply.

Of all the sciences, only mathematics deals with objects that cannot be perceived by our senses or detected by instruments of observation. The objects that advanced mathematics studies lie totally beyond the reach of the imagination. A schoolboy may think that the triangles or circles he studies in geometry are figures he can draw upon a piece of paper, but no perceptible figure, however carefully constructed with physical instruments, has the mathematical properties that can be demonstrated, but not visibly exhibited.

When the object being considered is an n-sided regular polygon, it is clear at once that it is an object of thought, not of perception or imagination. There are, of course, physical couples, triads, and quartets that exemplify the whole numbers 2, 3, and 4; but arithmetic goes far beyond positive integers to fractions, negative numbers, and imaginary ones, and to such objects as the square root of minus one.

Mathematics deals with ideal objects, not real things. That fact does not prevent mathematics from being applied to the world of physical things, and applied with extraordinary power that pays off in handsome practical results. Those branches of the natural and social sciences that apply mathematics, such as mathematical physics and econometrics or mathematical economics, are not only among the most exact, but are also the most fruitful in their production of results.

Like mathematics and unlike all the natural and social sciences, philosophy deals with ideal objects in the first instance. The ideas—the objects of thought—that we reflect upon when we start to philosophize lie beyond the reach of sense perception and imagination. That is why, like mathematics, philosophy can be described as "armchair thinking." No more than mathematics does it employ techniques of observation, experimentation, the gathering of data by empirical research, or an investigation of phenomena by means of apparatus or instruments. Like mathematics, it is not empirical or investigative.

Nevertheless, as in the case of mathematics, this fact does not prevent philosophy from being useful in thinking about experienced reality—about nature, human behavior, and social institutions. The better our understanding of ideas, especially the great ideas, the better we understand reality because of the light they throw on it.

So much, then, for the slur that ideas have nothing to do with reality. At least, so much for the moment; the rest of this book will provide ample evidence, I hope, that philosophy, like mathematics, is useful in our commerce with the experienced world.

When mathematics is applied to observable phenomena, its application is mediated by measurements made in other sciences, such as physics and economics. Philosophy's application to reality needs no such mediation. It is direct, without intervention by or dependence on quantified data that are required for the application of mathematics and that can be gathered only by the special observational techniques employed by the investigative sciences.

This explains why philosophy can be everybody's business, as the special sciences, including those that apply mathematics, are not. Precisely because it can be everybody's business, it should be part of everyone's general education.

Becoming acquainted and conversant with the great ideas will not prepare the individual for any special career—in business, the learned professions, or highly skilled occupations of one technical sort or another. Specialized schooling is required for that. But everyone is called to one common human vocation —that of being a good citizen and a thoughtful human being.

Only by the presence of philosophy in the general schooling of all is everyone prepared to discharge the obligations common to all because all are human beings. Schooling is essentially humanistic only to the extent that it is tinged with philosophy —with an introduction to the great ideas.

The tests that are employed to obtain some indication of the individual's aptitude for higher education include measurements of the range of his or her vocabulary. The size of a person's vocabulary, measured by the sheer number of words he or she is able to use correctly, is a very crude indication of mental development. While it may be true that a person with a very large vocabulary is one who manifests a wider acquaintance with literature or one who has greater facility with the written or spoken word, the mere size of the individual's vocabulary certainly does not reveal the breadth or depth of his mind—the scope of his understanding or the development of his ability to think.

In addition, the vocabulary questions included in what are called scholastic aptitude tests consist, for the most part, in quizzing the student about his acquaintance with the meaning of strange words, or at least words that are not frequently used in the give-and-take of everyday speech. It is far from clear what that is supposed to measure.

If the aim were to discover the student's familiarity with a specific branch of knowledge, one way to do that might be to test the individual's ability to use correctly a particular discipline's technical terms. This suggests the kind of vocabulary test that might be used to discover whether a student has the philosophical turn of mind that a good basic schooling would have given the individual if it were essentially humanistic, as it should be.

Unlike the words that usually appear in the vocabulary questions of scholastic aptitude tests, the words that name the great ideas are not strange words or words infrequently used in everyday speech. On the contrary, with few exceptions, they are as familiar and they are used as frequently as the most common words in the ordinary person's vocabulary. In fact, many of them are included in a vocabulary the reach of which does not extend beyond a thousand words.

This does not mean that a person with a vocabulary of this size and one that includes many or most of the words that name great ideas can use these words with a breadth or depth of meaning that manifests a well-grounded acquaintance with ideas or a sufficient understanding of them to render the world of his or her experience more intelligible.

The words that name the great ideas—none of them technical terms in any special science, all of them terms of common speech—constitute the basic vocabulary of philosophical thought, which is also to say the basic vocabulary of human thought. If philosophy is everybody's business, then not only should everyone be able to use these words correctly in a sentence when the standard of correctness is merely grammatical, but also everyone should be able to engage, to some extent, in intelligent discourse about the object of thought under consideration.

How much can the individual say, sequentially and coherently, when he is asked to consider one or another great idea? What questions is he able to ask about that object of thought? What answers can be given to these questions? Which answers hang together and which are opposed? What practical difference does it make whether we adopt one or another of the opposed answers? And how is one great idea related to others?

I am not sure I could construct a written test that would accurately measure an individual's conversancy with the great ideas. But I am relatively confident that I could conduct an oral examination that would give me a fairly clear indication of the philosophical breadth and depth of a person's mind—the range and reach of his understanding of the great ideas. I would do so by asking questions that pivoted about the words that name these ideas. It would be much better than the vocabulary tests now in use, for, by confining itself to the vocabulary of thought, it would measure more than mere linguistic facility; it would exhibit the stage of intellectual development the individual had attained.

The words that constitute the vocabulary of philosophical or human thought, I said earlier, would almost certainly be included in a vocabulary that numbered no more than a thousand words; perhaps as few as five hundred. *The Great Ideas, A Syntopicon* lists 102 such words. At the time some forty years ago when I was engaged in constructing the *Syntopicon,* I and my colleagues thought 102 was the number we needed in order to delineate the discussion of the great ideas that occurs in the great books of Western civilization. But now, with a different purpose in view, I think I can cut that number down to sixty-four, adding one or two as well as subtracting many.

My purpose now is to list the words that are not only in everyone's vocabulary, but that also name great ideas that everyone who has completed a basic, humanistic schooling should be reasonably conversant with. Only a few of the ideas I am going to name have emerged into prominence in modern times or have taken on special significance in the twentieth century. As Mark Twain correctly quipped, "The ancients stole all our ideas from us." Here, in alphabetical order, are the ones that should be in the possession of human beings at all times, but, perhaps, not in all places, because it must be acknowledged that they are characteristically Western ideas.

ANIMAL	HAPPINESS	PUNISHMENT
ART	HONOR	REASONING
BEAUTY	IMAGINATION	RELATION
BEING	JUDGMENT	RELIGION
CAUSE	JUSTICE	REVOLUTION
CHANCE	KNOWLEDGE	SENSE
CHANGE	LABOR	SIN
CITIZEN	LANGUAGE	SLAVERY
CONSTITUTION	LAW	SOUL
DEMOCRACY	LIBERTY (or FREEDOM)	SPACE
DESIRE	LIFE AND DEATH	STATE
DUTY	LOVE	TIME
EDUCATION	MAN	TRUTH
EMOTION	MATTER	TYRANNY
EQUALITY	MEMORY	VIOLENCE
EVOLUTION	MIND	VIRTUE AND VICE
EXPERIENCE	NATURE	WAR AND PEACE
FAMILY	OPINION	WEALTH
GOD	PLEASURE AND PAIN	WILL
GOOD AND EVIL	POETRY	WISDOM
GOVERNMENT	PROGRESS	WORLD
HABIT		

The list might be enlarged a little in the following manner. Under GOVERNMENT, we might place DEMOCRACY and TYRANNY. Under VIRTUE, we might place COURAGE, TEMPERANCE, and PRUDENCE. Under KNOWLEDGE, we might place HISTORY, MATHEMATICS, MEDICINE, PHILOSOPHY, SCIENCE, and THEOLOGY, and perhaps even ASTRONOMY, MECHANICS, and PHYSICS. Even with all these additions, the number would come to much less than a hundred.

Readers can cross-examine themselves—or, perhaps, members of their family or their friends—by asking, about each of the great ideas listed above, the kind of questions I suggested a little earlier. Unfortunately, this book cannot include what may be needed to determine whether the questions asked are correctly answered for all of the great ideas enumerated. But it will provide that for the six I have chosen to write about, and it will do a little more than that by relating the chosen six to quite a few others.

Why these six and where they stand in the overall pattern of the great ideas as they are related to one another, I will try to say in the next chapter.

CHAPTER 4

These Chosen Few

OUT OF SIXTY-FOUR GREAT IDEAS, all of them essential ingredients in the vocabulary of human thought, why just these—TRUTH, GOODNESS, and BEAUTY; LIBERTY, EQUALITY, and JUSTICE?

One answer jumps out of the page at us as we look at those six words. All, with the one exception of BEAUTY, are pivotal terms in the opening lines of the second paragraph of the Declaration of Independence: "We hold these truths . . ."; "all men are created equal"; "unalienable rights" (which, as we shall see, lie at the heart of justice); "among which are life, liberty . . ."; "deriving their just powers." And, if we understand "happiness" to consist in living a good human life, then "the pursuit of happiness" requires us to understand what makes a good life good.

In addition, if we turn to the Preamble of the Constitution of the United States, we find among the goals it sets for the government of this republic: establishing justice, securing the blessings of liberty, and promoting the general welfare (the word "welfare" like the word "happiness" requiring us to understand the idea of good).

Finally, there is the renewed pledge to these ideals that Lincoln uttered in his Gettysburg Address when he spoke of a nation "conceived in liberty and dedicated to the proposition that all men are created equal."

We observed in the preceding chapter that everyone is called to one common human vocation—that of being a good citizen and a thoughtful human being—and that, to discharge the obligation common to all human beings, schooling should be essentially humanistic, which is to say that it should provide at least an introduction to the great ideas and some measure of conversancy with them.

If that is so, with which of the great ideas should one begin? Or, to put it another way, which of the great ideas stand out as being of maximum importance for holding the high office of citizenship and performing its duties in a thoughtful manner? The answer is, certainly, ideas that we must understand in order to make our loyalty to the ideals of this republic more than empty lip service or, worse, blind acceptance of shibboleths.

An intelligent, thoughtful reading of the three prime documents that constitute the American testament turns on a better understanding than most of the graduates of our high schools and colleges now acquire, because basic schooling in this country has sorrowfully departed from the line of general and humanistic learning to which it should resolutely hew. That better understanding is certainly a minimal prerequisite to being a good citizen of this republic.

Putting aside for the moment the obligations of citizenship in a democracy, let us turn to the other element in the vocation common to all—the calling to become a thoughtful human being. This leads us to another answer to the question, Why these chosen few? That answer works somewhat differently for the first three of the six ideas and for the second three.

Two things can be said of both trios with equal accuracy. In both cases, the three ideas that are grouped together do, in fact, belong together; it would be extremely difficult to discuss any one of them adequately without reference to the other two. In both cases, one of the three associated ideas is the sovereign or governing one to which the other two owe some measure of subservience or obedience—truth in the one case, justice in the other.

A further point should, perhaps, be added. Each trio in its own way illuminates a large set of other ideas—ideas that also belong together. In the case of LIBERTY, EQUALITY, and JUSTICE, it is the trio as a whole that functions in this way. Not so in the case of TRUTH, GOODNESS, and BEAUTY. Here each of the three ideas by itself throws light on a set of related ideas.

It would be too much to say that these chosen few constitute the central source of light that illuminates the whole realm of great ideas—or at least all sixty-four of them named in the preceding chapter. But light is cast on a great many of them by the six I have chosen as a starting point for the exploration of the basic objects of human thought. How can a person become a truly thoughtful human being without engaging in that exploration? If so, what better place to begin?

In order to draw the lines of light that radiate from the chosen six to a large number of other ideas, it is necessary to recognize certain patterns of contexture inherent in the sixty or so great ideas that have been named—patterns that are concealed by a purely alphabetical arrangement of those ideas. An alphabetical arrangement of anything is a cowardly retreat from an intelligible ordering of the material.

Let us first consider the trio LIBERTY, EQUALITY, and JUSTICE, of which we said that it is the trio as a whole that throws light on other ideas. These three ideas are the ones we live by in society. They represent ideals which a considerable portion of the human race has sought to realize for themselves and their posterity.

The solitary individual, provided with a comfortable life on a tropical island, would not be moved to cry out for liberty, equality, and justice; nor would he have any occasion to engage in a struggle to achieve them for himself. Only in human society, in which the individual is associated both cooperatively and competitively with other human beings, is there any articulation of claims for liberty, equality, and justice, and only in society do individuals engage in the actions needed to support such claims.

The society may be that of the family or of the state—civil society, the political community. The claims made and the actions taken concern the institutions of society, especially the political institutions of the state, or civil society, and its economic arrangements as well.

These may or may not be just; these may or may not secure sufficient liberty for all; these may or may not provide an equality of conditions. The consideration of these matters involves the application of standards of justice to the laws of the state and especially to its underlying framework of law that is chartered in the constitution. It also bears on the qualifications for citizenship and on the distribution of wealth.

If we seek to understand government itself and the forms of government, especially the antithesis between constitutional government and despotism; if we are moved to consider the desirability of democracy and the threat it always faces from tyranny by the majority; if we recoil from slavery and other forms of human subjection; if we are concerned with violence and war as illnesses that weaken the fabric of society, while at the same time recognizing that revolutions, which may involve violence and war, are sometimes drastic expedients; if we hope for a peaceful resolution of the differences that bring men into conflict with one another—if we engage in thinking about these matters, we cannot get very far without finding that at every turn of thought we must have recourse to an understanding of LIBERTY and EQUALITY as well as JUSTICE.

Our understanding of those three great ideas thus radiates out to illuminate our consideration of many others. Ticked off in alphabetical order, they are: CITIZEN, CONSTITUTION, DEMOCRACY, FAMILY, GOVERNMENT, LAW, REVOLUTION, SLAVERY, STATE, TYRANNY, VIOLENCE, WAR AND PEACE, and WEALTH.

I turn now to the other trio: TRUTH, GOODNESS, and BEAUTY. These three ideas are the ones we judge by. Unlike the ideas we live by (LIBERTY, EQUALITY, and JUSTICE), these three function for us in our private as well as in our public life. The solitary individual enabled to live comfortably by himself or herself would still have occasion to judge something to be true or false, to appraise this to be good and that evil, to discriminate between the beautiful and the ugly.

Such judgments, appraisals, and discriminations may also occur, of course, when individuals are engaged in social interaction with one another. But quite apart from all the circumstances of social life, an individual's mind will not be able to avoid making such judgments, appraisals, and discriminations.

Thinking about LIBERTY, EQUALITY, and JUSTICE involves thinking about I and Thou—about the relationships between oneself and other human beings.

Thinking about TRUTH, GOODNESS, and BEAUTY involves, in the first instance at least, thinking about the whole world in which we live—about the knowledge we have of it, the desires it arouses in us, and the admiration it elicits from us. Here it is the relation of the self to everything else, not just other human beings, which is brought into focus.

I said earlier that, in recognizing the significance of TRUTH, GOODNESS, and BEAUTY, we must note how each of the three ideas by itself throws light on a set of related ideas. Let us now see how that works out.

We cannot understand the difference between knowledge and opinion without being aware of how each is related to truth. The truth to be found in poetry is not the same as the truth we look for in history, science, or philosophy. The criteria of what is true and false, and the devices we employ to test the truth of anything that is proposed for our affirmation or denial, vary as we pass from mathematics to the empirical sciences, from the empirical sciences to philosophy, and from philosophy to theology and religion.

The very act of making judgments is an act that asserts something to be true or false. The character of the judgments we make—whether judgments that something is or is not the case, or judgments that something ought or ought not to be—cannot be understood without seeking an answer to a fundamental question about radically different modes of truth.

We must also ask whether truth exists only in judgments of the mind or also in statements we make when we use language; whether there is truth in the senses, the memory, and the imagination, as well as in the mind; whether the kind of truth that makes our reasoning valid is the same kind of truth as that which makes our judgments sound; whether appeal to experience is always an ultimate test of truth.

Here, then, ticked off in alphabetical order, are the ideas that our understanding of TRUTH helps us to understand a little better: EXPERIENCE, IMAGINATION, JUDGMENT, KNOWLEDGE, LANGUAGE, MEMORY, MIND, OPINION, POETRY, REASONING, RELIGION; to which we might add the ideas that are related to knowledge and opinion—MATHEMATICS, PHILOSOPHY, SCIENCE, THEOLOGY.

The idea of GOODNESS has its own sphere of influence. We cannot think of the good without thinking of the desirable, or of the desirable without thinking of the good. One of our most frequent uses of the word *good* is in such phrases as "a good man," "a good will," and "a good life." Our understanding of what is meant involves our understanding of the virtues as good habits, proceeding from a good will, and of happiness, or a good life, as one that is enriched by the possession of all good things, among which certainly are wealth, honor, the love of friends and family, a decent amount of pleasure and avoidance of pain, knowledge and especially wisdom, not to mention a healthy life, liberty, equality, and the supporting conditions provided by a good society—one that is just and peaceful.

Once again ticked off in alphabetical order, here are the ideas on which our understanding of GOODNESS throws light: DESIRE, FAMILY, HABIT, HAPPINESS, HONOR, LIFE (a healthy one), LOVE, MAN, PLEASURE AND PAIN, VIRTUE AND VICE (perhaps also SIN), and WILL. One might go a bit farther and add EMOTION because it is involved in the effort of the will to be good and to form the good habits that are the virtues; and if SIN is touched on, then perhaps we may not be able to avoid questions about the goodness of GOD and about man's goodness in relation to GOD. In addition to all of these, we cannot fail to note that the consideration of GOODNESS relates to ideas already mentioned in other connections: not only KNOWLEDGE and PEACE, but also the great ideas that comprise the other trio: LIBERTY, EQUALITY, and JUSTICE.

BEAUTY has the smallest circle of related ideas the understanding of which it affects. We expect to find beauty in works of art and poetry, especially the products of the arts that are sometimes called "fine arts" in contrast to "useful arts," and sometimes *beaux arts,* or arts of the beautiful. We also expect to find it in the things of nature. Beauty, like goodness, is thought to inhere in objects that we desire or love. It affords us a certain experience of pleasure, one that occurs in the sphere of our knowing (knowing that involves the senses, the imagination, and the mind) rather than in the sphere of our actions. Thus, the other great ideas, in alphabetical order, to which BEAUTY relates are: ART, DESIRE (perhaps also EMOTION), EXPERIENCE, IMAGINATION, KNOWLEDGE, LOVE, MIND, PLEASURE AND PAIN, POETRY, and SENSE.

The reader who carefully examines all the lines of light or strands of influence that delineate the bearing of the chosen six on other great ideas will see that, of the two trios, the first is the more fundamental. It dominates the second. The values it encompasses are transcendant and universal, applicable to everything. That is why we will begin with it, devoting Part Two of this book to the ideas we judge by (TRUTH, GOODNESS, and BEAUTY) and then going on, in Part Three, to the ideas we live by and act on (LIBERTY, EQUALITY, and JUSTICE).

In the chapters of Parts Two and Three that lie ahead, I will attempt to say no more about each of the ideas under consideration than will recommend itself to common sense as worthy of assent without reliance upon the intricate subtleties of analysis or argument. There is, of course, more to say. A great idea is almost always one about which challenging questions have been raised. The great philosophical questions are, for the most part, questions about the great ideas.

These questions, which have been disputed by those who have devoted their lives to philosophical thought, require more protracted and profound reflection than is appropriate in an introductory exploration such as this. However, there may be readers who wish to push farther in their thinking than this book carries them. For them, I have appended, in Part Four, an epilogue that presents questions they may wish to ponder and issues on which they may attempt either to take sides or to suspend judgment.

PART TWO

Ideas We Judge By: Truth, Goodness, and Beauty

CHAPTER 5

The Liar and the Skeptic

IT IS POSSIBLE TO BE EITHER A LIAR OR A SKEPTIC, but not both. Of course, it is also possible, and quite preferable, to be neither.

The person who maintains that he knows nothing because nothing is knowable, or who declares that no statement can be either true or false, interdicts himself from telling lies. His extreme skepticism removes him from the ordinary world in which most of us live and in which, according to him, we live under the illusion that we can discriminate between statements that are true and statements that are false.

Illusion or not, the liar at least thinks that he knows the difference between what is true and what is false when he deliberately deceives someone about a matter of fact. If he were in total ignorance of the fact in question, or in grave doubt about it, he could not tell a lie.

Consider the dishonest jeweler who persuades his customer to purchase a ring that he claims is set with a diamond of high quality, aware that what he is offering is nothing but a relatively worthless imitation of the genuine article. He has told a deliberate lie, which he simply could not do if, like the skeptic, he were to think that the statement he made—"The stone in this ring is a diamond"—could be neither true nor false, because nothing is either true or false.

However, there is one lie that the skeptic can tell. Sincere in his adherence to skepticism, he can still deceive someone else by pretending not to be a skeptic. Instead of honestly confessing his skepticism, he can verbally declare the very opposite, saying that he thinks some statements are true and others false when he really thinks no such thing at all.

This pinpoints for us the essence of lying. It consists in putting into words the very opposite of what one really thinks— the opposite of one's own state of mind. If your landlord thinks that rents are not going up and tells you in so many words that they are, he has lied to you. The lie must, of course, be intentional and with a deliberate purpose to deceive for the sake of gaining some advantage, regardless of the injury that may result to the person who is deceived.

The condemnation of lying as morally wrong or unjust presupposes that injury results from the deception. What we call a "white lie" and usually condone rather than condemn consists in a harmless deception or one that even may work to the benefit of the person deceived. But whether the false statement turns out to be injurious or beneficial, it remains a false statement because what its words say do not correspond to what the person who has made the statement actually thinks.

The truth of verbally expressed statements thus consists in their correspondence or agreement with the state of mind of the person making them or, if you will, with the statements he or she makes in the privacy of his or her own mind. A verbally expressed statement is false if the opposite relation obtains between it and what the person who makes it thinks, or says to himself—if the two do not agree or correspond, as is the case if I tell you that I have a toothache when I do not.

To speak falsely, it has been pointed out, consists in willfully misplacing one's ontological predicates. That is a highfalutin way of saying that to speak falsely consists in putting "is" where one should put "is not," or "is not" where one should put "is." The dishonest jeweler asserted, "This *is* a diamond," when he should have said, "This *is not* a diamond," because he was aware that it was not what he asserted it to be.

When we characterize a person as a liar, implying thereby a condemnation of his or her moral character, we usually impute to that person a habitual disposition or inclination to speak falsely whenever some profit can be gained from the deception. We are put on guard to beware of what that person says. It is more likely than not to be false and result in an injury to someone.

Without being chronic or habitual liars, who among us would not confess to having told some lies, white or otherwise? By that confession, we separate ourselves from the extreme skeptic who finds it impossible to tell lies, except, perhaps, the one lie that attempts to conceal his skeptical state of mind. Unlike the extreme skeptic, we do not refuse to attribute truth to certain statements and falsity to others, sometimes with more assurance, sometimes with less. The statements we regard as true are those that not only honestly express what we think to be the case, but those that in our judgment also assert what is in fact the case.

Here, too, there is a relationship of agreement or correspondence, but now that relation obtains between what a person thinks, believes, opines, or says to himself and what actually exists or does not exist in reality. When I assert that that which is, is, or that that which is not, is not, my assertion is true. When I assert that that which is, is not, or that that which is not, is, my assertion is false.

Just as the truth of speech consists in the agreement or correspondence between what one says to another and what one thinks or says to oneself, so the truth of thought consists in the agreement or correspondence between what one thinks, believes, or opines and what actually exists or does not exist in the reality that is independent of our minds and of our thinking one thing or another.

This definition of truth answers the question, "What is truth?" but about any particular opinion or belief that we may harbor in our minds, it does not answer the question, "Is it true?" That is a much harder question to answer, even for those who accept the definition of truth as consisting in an agreement or correspondence between the mind and reality. For the extreme skeptic who rejects that definition on the ground that it erroneously presupposes a state of reality with which a state of mind can agree or disagree, that second question is not merely harder than the first, but unanswerable.

The definition of truth involves an erroneous presupposition, the skeptic charges. Does not his use of the word "erroneously" trip him up? Has he not contradicted himself by saying, on the one hand, that nothing is either true or false and yet saying, on the other hand, that the presupposition involved in the definition of truth is an erroneous presupposition or, in other words, false?

We are verging here on an age-old reply to the extreme skeptic that dismisses him as refuting himself. One cannot say that no statements are true or false, or that there is no such thing as truth in the sense defined, without contradicting oneself. If the statement that expresses the skeptic's view about truth is one that he himself regards as true, then at least one statement is true. If it is false, then it is quite possible for many other statements to be either true or false. If the statement that expresses the skeptic's view is neither true nor false, then why should we pay any attention to what he says?

Either he has contradicted himself or he has impelled us to discontinue any further conversation with him on the grounds that it can lead nowhere. There is no point in talking to some-one who is willing to answer any question by saying both yes and no at the same time.

Since the extreme skeptic does not acknowledge the restraint imposed by the rule of reason that we ought not to contradict ourselves if we can avoid doing so, our refutation of him by appealing to that rule does not silence him. He has no objection to being unreasonable. We may have refuted him to our own satisfaction, but that does not carry with it an acknowledgment by him that he has been refuted and should abandon his skep-ticism. The only consequence that follows from our regarding his view as self-contradictory and therefore self-refuting is the judgment we may be forced to make that there is no point in carrying on the conversation with him any further.

The commonsense view is the one that all of us embrace when we reject the self-contradictory and self-refuting position of the extreme skeptic as being not only unreasonable, but also impracticable. There is hardly an aspect of our daily lives that would be the same if we were to embrace instead of rejecting the position of the extreme skeptic. We are firmly committed to the view that truth and falsity are ascertainable by us and that, with varying degrees of assurance, we can somehow discrimi-nate between what is true and what is false. Almost everything we do or rely upon is grounded in that commitment.

One illustration of this should suffice. We accept trial by jury before a judicial tribunal as a way of deciding disputed ques-tions of fact. Was the prisoner at the bar seen running away from the scene of the crime? Was the last will and testament of the deceased signed by him while in a sound state of body and mind? Witnesses are called to give testimony in answer to such questions; and, in the direct and cross-examination of the wit-nesses, the attempt is made by counsel either to enhance their credibility in the eyes of the jury or to diminish it.

When all the evidence is in and the jury has completed its deliberations, the verdict they render asserts the truth of a statement of fact, either beyond a reasonable doubt in a criminal prosecution or by a preponderance of the evidence in a civil litigation.

That's what the word "verdict" means—the assertion of a truth. The verdict that the prisoner at the bar is not guilty as charged may spring from the jury's low estimate of the credibility of the witness who testified that he saw the person charged with murder running away from the scene of the crime. The verdict may also have been determined by more credible testimony that he was somewhere else on that occasion. It never occurs to the jury to doubt that one of the two alternatives must be the case in fact: Either the person charged with the crime did have the opportunity to commit it or he did not have the opportunity to commit it.

The presupposition called erroneous by the skeptic will not be regarded as such by persons holding a commonsense view of the world in which we live. Common sense would not hesitate for a moment to assert that at a given time a particular thing either exists or does not exist, that a certain event either occurred or did not occur, that something being considered either does or does not have a certain characteristic or attribute. Far from being an outrageous, not to say erroneous, assumption about the reality to which our beliefs or opinions may or may not correspond, this view of reality seems undeniable to common sense.

By the commonsense view with regard to truth, I mean simply the nonskeptical view that understands what truth consists in—what it means for a statement to be true rather than false. In addition, the commonsense view does not doubt that some statements are true and others false and that there are ways of finding out which is which.

Without being explicitly aware of it, the jury embraces this commonsense view in its unquestioning acceptance of the fact that the person charged with murder either did or did not have the opportunity to commit the crime. That being so, then one or the other of these alternatives must be true and the other false. The grounds of the jury's verdict are thus seen to consist, first, in their accepting the presupposition involved in the definition of truth, which the skeptic rejects as erroneous; and, second, in their confidence that by weighing the evidence they can ascertain which of two opposite statements is true and which is false.

In the first instance, they implicitly acknowledge the correctness of the definition of truth as an agreement or correspondence between the mind and reality, which means that they affirm the existence of a reality that is independent of the mind and is what it is regardless of what we may think about it.

In the second instance, they implicitly acknowledge that, in addition to knowing what truth consists in, they can also use their minds to discover whether a given statement is true or false.

Human beings have been charged with perjury and convicted of it. They have been found guilty of falsification when they are under oath to speak the truth, the whole truth, and nothing but the truth. If the skeptic's denials were sound, the oath every witness is required to take, and the threat of a prosecution for perjury if he or she fails to live up to it, would be a scandalous travesty.

Judicial procedure and trial by jury afford but one example out of many, all of which tend to show how in the practical affairs of daily life the commonsense view prevails—in business and commerce, in the practice of the professions, in the rearing of children and in other aspects of family life, in the consideration of the claims made by candidates for public office, or the claims made by advertisers, in buying and selling and in economic transactions of every sort, and in all our dealings with our fellow human beings.

In our further consideration of truth in the chapters to follow, we shall be concerned with the failure to speak the truth that arises from ignorance or error rather than from deliberate prevarication. One does not have the truth in one's mind and so, with no intention to deceive, one fails to speak it when one expresses one's mind in verbal utterance.

There is a clear difference between the judgment that what a man says is false and the judgment that he is telling a lie. His statement may be false without his necessarily being a liar. Try as he will to speak truthfully by saying precisely what he thinks, he may be mistaken in what he says through error or ignorance.

The person we ask for directions may honestly but erroneously think that a certain road is the shortest route to the destination we wish to reach. When he tells us which road to take, what he says is false, but not a lie. However, if he does in fact know another road to be shorter and withholds that information from us, then his statement is not only false, but also a lie.

CHAPTER 6

Milder Forms of Skepticism

READERS WILL HAVE NOTED that, in the preceding chapter, I referred to the skepticism there being considered as extreme. Skepticism takes milder or more moderate forms.

Of these, three in particular deserve our attention because they are widely prevalent and affect our understanding of truth. Two of the three tend to involve mistakes that should be avoided, but the third is that measure of sound skepticism that wisdom urges us to adopt.

Pyrrho, a philosopher of antiquity, has been regarded as the outstanding exponent of extreme skepticism, and so in the history of Western thought extreme skepticism bears the label "Pyrrhonism." In modern times, the philosopher David Hume attempted to draw a line between Pyrrhonism—the extreme skepticism that sensible persons are compelled to reject—and that moderate form of skepticism that wisdom recommends.

"The great subverter of *Pyrrhonism* or the excessive principles of scepticism," Hume declared, "is action, and employment, and the occupations of common life.

These principles may flourish and triumph in the schools; where it is, indeed, difficult, if not impossible, to refute them. But as soon as they leave the shade, and by the presence of the real objects, which actuate our passions and sentiments, are put in opposition to the more powerful principles of our nature, they vanish like smoke, and leave the most determined sceptic in the same condition as other mortals.

Hence, Hume concluded,

A Pyrrhonian cannot expect, that his philosophy will have any constant influence on the mind: or if it had, that its influence would be beneficial to society. On the contrary, he must acknowledge, if he will acknowledge anything, that all human life must perish, were his principles universally and steadily to prevail. All discourse, all action would immediately cease; and men remain in a total lethargy, till the necessities of nature, unsatisfied, put an end to their miserable existence.

The "more mitigated" or moderate skepticism that Hume recommended as "both durable and useful," he also thought results from the correction of extreme skepticism by common sense and by reflection. It consists in an ever-present tincture or tinge of doubt that should accompany all—or, if not all, most —of the judgments we make concerning what is true or false. It should arise from our acknowledgment of the infirmities—and the consequent fallibility—of the human mind. It holds a middle ground between what Hume calls excessive skepticism at one extreme and excessive dogmatism at the other, a dogmatism that claims certitude and infallibility about matters in which neither is attainable.

Before we consider how this form of skepticism affects our understanding of truth, I would like to deal briefly with the other two forms, which tend to involve mistakes that can and should be avoided. One is the mistake that people make when they misinterpret the familiar remark: "That may be true for you, but not for me." The other is an equally widespread misinterpretation of the remark: "That may have been true sometime ago, but no longer."

The first of these misinterpretations arises from the failure to distinguish between the truth or falsity that inheres in a proposition or statement and the judgment that a person makes with regard to the truth or falsity of the statement in question. We may differ in our judgment about what is true, but that does not affect the truth of the matter itself.

Let us take, for example, a difference of opinion about the number of peaks in the Colorado Rockies that exceed 14,000 feet. One person sets the number at fifty; the other says, "Not so." The number of peaks in Colorado exceeding 14,000 feet is some definite integer, and so the statement that sets it at fifty is either true or false, regardless of what the persons who dispute this matter of fact may think about it.

The truth or falsity of a statement derives from its relation to the ascertainable facts, not from its relation to the judgments that human beings make. I may affirm as true a statement that is in fact false. You may deny as false a statement that is in fact true. My affirmation and your denial in no way alter or affect the truth or falsity of the statements that you and I have wrongly judged. We do not make statements true or false by affirming or denying them. They have truth or falsity regardless of what we think, what opinions we hold, what judgments we make.

A different jury hearing the evidence in a particular case might reach a different verdict. Though the prisoner at the bar may be thought guilty in the eyes of one jury and innocent in the eyes of another, one of those verdicts is right and the other wrong because the prisoner is either guilty or not guilty as charged. If guilty, then a verdict that declares the prisoner's guilt is true even when a jury renders the opposite verdict.

The mistake of identifying the truth or falsity of a statement with our attribution of truth or falsity to it can be easily corrected. Those who persist in the mistake turn truth and falsity into an entirely subjective affair. They are, in effect, espousing the position that what's true for me is true, and that's all there is to it.

Stated another way, they are maintaining that there is no truth at all apart from what is true for me or true for you. When what is true for me is not true for you, I may try to change your opinion and win you over to mine, but even if I do succeed in persuading you that mine is correct, we are together no nearer to the truth in any objective sense than we were when we differed.

The subjective aspect of truth lies in the claim that the individual makes for the veracity of his judgment. The objective aspect lies in the agreement or correspondence between what an individual believes or opines and the reality about which he is making a judgment when he holds a certain belief or opinion. The objective aspect is the primary one.

To ignore it, or to fail to see that it is distinct from the subjective aspect, washes out the meaning of the word "true." This is precisely what happens when an individual who claims that a certain statement is true for him adds, "And that's all there is to it." He might just as well have said of the statement he calls true that he likes it, and that's all there is to it.

The form of skepticism that we have been examining is sometimes referred to as "subjectivism" and sometimes as "relativism." It is widely prevalent even among persons who would not regard themselves as addicted to skepticism because they do not think of themselves as adopting the extreme skeptical view that nothing is either true or false. But they have, nevertheless, allowed themselves to fall back into excessive skepticism by their refusal to acknowledge that subjective differences of opinion concerning what is true or false can be resolved by efforts to ascertain what is objectively true or false, remembering that the truth of a statement resides in its relation to reality, not in its relation to the individual's judgment about it.

Closely akin is the form of skepticism—or relativism—that

makes the truth of a statement depend upon the circumstances of time and place. Everyone is acquainted with such remarks as "That may have been true in the Middle Ages, but it is no longer true," or "That may be true for primitive people, but it is not true for us." The mistake here is exactly the same mistake as before.

A portion of the human race some centuries ago held it to be true that the earth is flat. That false opinion has now been generally repudiated. This should not be interpreted to mean that the objective truth has changed—that what once was true is no longer true. If it is now objectively true that this planet is spherical, it never was true that it is flat. What has changed is not the truth of the matter but the prevalence of an opinion that has ceased to be popular.

Another example may help to make this clear. The population of a country changes from time to time, but a statement about the size of a country's population at a given time remains true when, at a later time, it has increased in size. The presence of the date in a statement about the population of the United States in a certain year enables that statement to remain true forever, if it was accurate in the first place.

"Forever" is a long time and "immutable" is a strong word, and yet it must be said that if a given statement is ever objectively true, it is true forever and immutably true. The impulse to recoil from what many may be inclined to regard as an outrageous claim can be checked by remembering that the claim does not preclude acknowledging that our judgments about what is true or false change from time to time, as well as differing from place to place. What is mutable and variable with the circumstances of time and place are the opinions we hold concerning the true and the false, not what is objectively true and false.

Sometimes the change is only in our minds and not in reality, nor in the relation between that unchanging reality and statements we make about it. Sometimes reality itself changes, as when a new species of living organism comes into existence or an existent species becomes extinct. But a statement to the effect that a species now extinct existed in an earlier geological era, as evidenced by its fossil remains in a certain stratum of the earth's crust, remains immutably true (if true in the first place). The fact that the species no longer exists does not impeach the accuracy of the statement about its existence at an earlier time.

The subjectivism and relativism we have been considering are much more prevalent in regard to goodness and beauty than they are with regard to truth. One reason for this may be that it is easier to correct the errors involved in the case of truth. It is easier to distingish between the objective and subjective aspects of truth. We will find that more difficult to do when we come to the discussion of goodness and beauty.

With regard to goodness and beauty, all of us are familiar with the dictates of subjectivism and relativism: "There is nothing good or evil but thinking makes it so" and "Beauty is entirely in the eye of the beholder." But with regard to goodness and beauty as well as with regard to truth, it is necessary to distinguish between the objective and subjective aspects in order to prevent the relapse into extreme skepticism that results from an uncorrected and unrestrained subjectivism and relativism.

Let me recapitulate before going on. Individuals differ from one another in their judgments concerning what is true. Each by himself or herself differs from time to time in what he believes or holds to be true. We have all said, "That's true for me even though it may not be true for you," and "I once thought that to be true but I no longer do." Properly interpreted, such remarks do not obliterate the objectivity of truth. On the contrary, they appeal to it, for if truth were entirely subjective we would have no basis for trying to resolve by rational means our differences of opinion about what is true; nor would we have any basis for congratulating ourselves on having made an advance by replacing a false opinion with a true one.

It is with all this in mind that the third of the milder forms of skepticism—the only one that is entirely sound—turns our attention away from the objective aspect of truth, the existence of which it does not question. Looking at the subjective aspect of truth, it offers us a correct interpretation of our conflicting and changing judgments concerning what is true or false. The fact that we differ in our judgments and change them from time to time should awaken us to the wisdom of a cautious restraint— not to regard our judgments as certain and secure, as infallible and incorrigible.

The fact that we often disagree with one another's judgments about what is true and the fact that we often repudiate an earlier judgment and replace it later by one that is quite contrary to it should persuade us of the infirmity, frailty, and fallibility of the human mind in its efforts to get at the truth. Being persuaded of this should not lead us to abandon those efforts as entirely futile or fruitless, but it should restrain us from claiming certitude, finality, and incorrigibility for judgments that are subject to doubt, change, and correction.

The objective truth of a statement may be immutable, but not our subjective judgment about whether it is true. There are no degrees of objective truth. A statement is either true or false objectively. But when, subjectively, we judge a statement to be true or false, we may do so with more or less assurance, and accordingly we may speak of it as being more or less true, or we may say that the probability of its being true is greater or less.

The form of skepticism that wisdom recommends we adopt is one that does not challenge the objectivity of truth, but it does enjoin us to recognize how few are the judgments concerning what is true for which we can rightly claim certitude and finality, and how many fall in the realm of doubt where they are subject to change and correction by all the means that human beings employ in their efforts to get at the truth. In fact, it is only in the realm of doubt that we engage in the pursuit of truth.

CHAPTER 7

The Realm of Doubt

WHEN SHOULD WE SAY, "I know," and do so with complete assurance? When, after expressing a judgment, are we warranted in adding, "This is something that I know beyond the shadow of a doubt"?

When instead, with something less than complete assurance and yet not without some basis for our judgment, should we say, "I believe," "I think," "I have the opinion that . . ." or use such phrases as "in my judgment" or "in my opinion"? When, after expressing a judgment, should we add the comment: "This is something I have reason to believe is true"?

The criteria for drawing the line that divides the realm of certitude from the realm of doubt can be stated abstractly. As so stated, the criteria are not difficult to understand. Difficulties arise only when we try to apply these criteria to particular cases in an attempt to decide which of our judgments belong in the realm of certitude and which in the realm of doubt.

The criteria are as follows. A judgment belongs in the realm of certitude when it is of the sort that (1) cannot be challenged by the consideration of new evidence that results from additional or improved observations, nor (2) can it be criticized by improved reasoning or the detection of inadequacies or errors in the reasoning we have done. Beyond challenge or criticism, such judgments are indubitable, or beyond doubt.

In contrast, a judgment is subject to doubt if there is any possibility at all (1) of its being challenged in the light of additional or more accurate observations or (2) of its being criticized on the basis of more cogent or more comprehensive reasoning.

Let me illustrate this by reference once again to judicial proof in a jury trial of issues of fact. In criminal prosecutions, the degree of proof required is defined as being "beyond a reasonable doubt." But this does not take the verdict rendered by the jury out of the realm of doubt.

What the jury is asked to bring in is a verdict that they have no reason to doubt—no rational basis for doubting—in the light of all the evidence offered and the arguments presented by opposing counsel.

It always remains possible that new evidence may be forthcoming and, if that occurs, the case may be reopened and a new trial may result in a different verdict. It also remains possible for the verdict to be appealed to a higher court on the grounds of procedural errors that affected the weighing of the evidence in the deliberations of the jury.

The original verdict may have been beyond a reasonable doubt at the time it was made, but it is not indubitable—not beyond all doubt or beyond the shadow of a doubt—precisely because it can be challenged by new evidence or set aside by an appeal that calls attention to procedural errors that may have invalidated the jury's deliberations—the reasoning they did in weighing and interpreting the evidence presented.

In civil litigation, the degree of proof required is defined as being "by a preponderance of the evidence." Here the jury's verdict claims no more than that the answer it gives to a question of fact has greater probability than the opposite answer. As the jurors have interpreted and weighed the evidence, they have found that it tends to favor one answer rather than another. Here, as in a criminal prosecution, additional evidence or better thinking on the jury's part might result in a different verdict. The balance might shift in the opposite direction.

In the affairs of daily life, many of the judgments we make are, like jury verdicts, beyond a reasonable doubt or are favored by a preponderance of the evidence. For all practical purposes, we regard judgments of the first sort as being so highly probable that we act on them as if they were certain. We need not hesitate to act on them even though new evidence may be forthcoming in the future or a flaw in our thinking may be discovered. In the light of all the evidence we have before us and the thinking we have done, we have no reason at present to doubt the truth of such judgments. But we should always remember that that does not make them indubitable; that does not give them the kind of certitude that removes them from the realm of doubt.

The essential difference between genuine certitude and the substitute for it that is often called "moral certainty" or "practical certainty" lies in the finality and incorrigibility of indubitable judgments. Even when we act on a highly probable judgment as if it were a certainty for all practical purposes, it remains a judgment that is subject to correction, to challenge, and to criticism. It is one about which we may in the future think it reasonable to change our minds.

In a wide variety of daily affairs—in the conduct of family life, in the care of our bodies and in all matters of health and disease, in our business or professional careers, in our financial dealings, especially in making investments, in our political decisions, especially with regard to foreign policy and international relations—we frequently act on judgments that are not beyond a reasonable doubt, but are simply more probable than their opposites. In the light of the evidence available at the time and in the light of the best thinking we have done so far, we regard them as more likely to be true.

The critical caution we must exercise is contained in the words "at the time" and "so far." These words remind us that the future always holds the possibility of additional evidence and better thinking, either of which may shift the weight of. probability in the opposite direction.

The realm of doubt is the realm of judgments that have a future, for better or for worse. This is not so in the case of judgments that have the finality and incorrigibility of certitude.

If we turn now from judgments that we make in the practical affairs of daily life to the conclusions of historical research, to the findings, hypotheses, and theories of the investigative sciences, and even to certain branches of mathematics, the same criteria function to place in the realm of doubt a fairly large portion of what these learned disciplines offer us as knowledge. This assessment may appear shocking to those who, distinguishing between knowledge on the one hand and opinion or belief on the other hand, regard history, science, and mathematics as branches of organized knowledge, not as collections of mere opinions or beliefs.

The world "knowledge" for them has the connotation of truth; in fact, it is inseparable from it. There cannot be false knowledge, as there can be false opinions and beliefs. The phrase "true knowledge" is redundant; the phrase "false knowledge" is self-contradictory.

However, those who hold this view acknowledge that there is progress in these disciplines. They as well as everyone else speak of the advancement of learning in all these fields. They attribute it to new discoveries, improved observations, the development of sounder hypotheses, the substitution of more comprehensive theories for less comprehensive ones, more elaborate and more precise analysis or interpretation of the data at hand, and rectified or more rigorous reasoning. Less adequate formulations are replaced by better ones—better because they are thought more likely to be true, or nearer to the truth being sought and, therefore, better approximations of it.

In short, all these branches of organized knowledge have a future, a future they would not have if the present found them in possession of judgments about what is true or false that had finality and incorrigibility. To whatever extent history, science, and mathematics have a future, to that same extent these bodies of "knowledge" belong in the realm of doubt, not in the realm of certitude.

I put the word "knowledge" in quotation marks because the word has two meanings, not one. The same holds for the word "opinion." The recognition of the two senses in which we use these words will overcome the shock initially experienced by those who recoiled from locating history, science, and mathematics in the realm of doubt, because they are accustomed to regarding them as branches of knowledge, not as collections of opinions or beliefs.

Let us first consider the meaning of the word "knowledge" that has already been mentioned. It is the sense in which knowledge cannot be false and, therefore, has the infallibility, finality, and incorrigibility that are attributes of judgments in the realm of certitude. Let us call this the strong sense of the term.

At the opposite extreme from knowledge in this strong sense is opinion in the weak sense of that term. When we use the word "opinion" in this sense, we refer to judgments on our part that are no more than personal predilections or prejudices. We have no basis for them, either empirical or rational. We cannot support them by appeal to carefully accumulated evidence or by appeal to reasoning that gives them credibility. We do not, in short, have sufficient reason for claiming that they are more likely to be true than are their opposites.

We prefer the opinions to which we are attached on emotional, not rational, grounds. Our attachment to them is arbitrary and voluntary—an act of will on our part, whatever its causes may be. Since we may just as capriciously adopt the opposite view, unfounded opinions of this sort fall to the lowest level of the realm of doubt.

In between these two extremes lie judgments that can be called knowledge in the weak sense of that term and opinion in the strong sense of that term. Here we have judgments that are neither arbitrary nor voluntary, judgments we have rational grounds for adopting, judgments the probability of which we can appraise in the light of all the evidence available at the moment and in the light of the best thinking we can do—the best analysis and interpretation we can make of that evidence, again at the moment.

At the moment! The future holds in store the possibility of additional or improved evidence and amplified or rectified reasoning. That fact, as we have seen, places such judgments in the realm of doubt. They have the aspect of opinion because they may turn out to be false rather than true, but they also have the aspect of knowledge because, *at the moment,* we have no reason to doubt them. They are beyond reasonable doubt, but not beyond that shadow of a doubt, from which they cannot escape because they have a future.

Readers who have followed the argument so far may begin to wonder whether the realm of certitude is a completely empty domain. If not, what sort of judgments can we expect to find there?

The answer I am about to give applies not only to judgments we make in the course of our daily lives, judgments ordinarily made by persons of common sense, even the judgments such persons may come to make when their common sense is enlightened by philosophical reflection. It also applies to judgments in the field of mathematics and in some, if not all, of the empirical sciences.

Truths called self-evident provide the most obvious examples of knowledge in the strong sense of that term. They are called self-evident because our affirmation of them does not depend on evidence marshaled in support of them nor upon reasoning designed to show that they are conclusions validly reached by inference. We recognize their truth immediately or directly from our understanding of what they assert. We are convinced —convinced, not persuaded—of their truth because we find it impossible to think the opposite of what they assert. We are in no sense free to think the opposite.

Self-evident truths are not tautologies, trifling and uninstructive, such as the statement "All triangles have three sides." A triangle being defined as a three-sided figure, we learn nothing from that statement. Contrast it with the statement, "No triangle has any diagonals," which is both self-evident and instructive, not a tautology.

The self-evidence of the truth of the latter statement derives immediately from our understanding of the definition of a triangle as a three-sided figure and from our understanding of the definition of a diagonal as a straight line drawn between two nonadjacent angles. Seeing at once that a triangle contains no nonadjacent angles, we see at once that no diagonals can be drawn in a triangle.

Our understanding of diagonals also enables us to see at once that the number of diagonals that can be drawn in a plane figure that is a regular polygon having n sides (where n stands for any whole number) is the number of sides multiplied by three less than that number, the product being then divided by two.

Sometimes, as in the case of "No triangle has any diagonals," the self-evidence of the truth derives from our understanding of definitions. Sometimes, it derives from our understanding of terms that are not only undefined but are also indefinable, such as "part" and "whole."

Since we cannot understand what a part is without reference to a whole, or understand what a whole is without reference to parts, we cannot define parts and wholes. Nevertheless, our understanding of parts and wholes makes it impossible for us to think that, in the case of a physical body, its parts are greater than the whole. That the whole body is always greater than any of its parts is not only true, but self-evident.

Equally self-evident is the truth that nothing can both exist and not exist at the same time; or that, at a given time, it can both have and not have a certain characteristic. Our understanding of what it means for anything to act on another or be acted upon gives us another self-evident truth. Only that which actually exists can act upon another and that other can be acted upon only if it also actually exists. A merely possible shower of rain cannot drench anyone; nor can I be protected from the rain by a merely possible umbrella.

How about the prime example of self-evident truth proposed in the Declaration of Independence—that all men are created equal? Clearly, it is not self-evident as stated if the word "created" is understood to mean *created by God,* for the existence of God and God's act of creation require the support of reasoning —reasoning that can be challenged. Suppose, however, that the proposition had been "All men are by nature equal." On what understanding of the terms involved might that statement be regarded as self-evidently true?

First of all, we do understand "equal" to mean "neither more nor less." If, then, we understand "all men by nature" to mean "all human beings" or "all members of the same species," it becomes self-evidently true for us that all are equal, which is to say that no human being is more or less human than any other.

All persons have, in some degree, whatever properties belong to all members of the species *Homo sapiens.* The inequality of one individual with another lies in the degree to which this or that specific property is possessed, but not in the degree of humanity that is common to all.

I have dwelled at some length on this example not only because we will have to return to it in later chapters dealing with the idea of equality, but also because the proposition about the equality of all human beings may have to be defended against those who advance the opposite view—Aristotle, for example, who maintains that some human beings are by nature born to be free, and some are by nature born to be slaves; or the male chauvinists over centuries past, and even in the present, who believe that females are inferior human beings.

I think the truth of the proposition about human equality can be defended against all these errors, but a self-evident truth should need no defense whatsoever. Hence the proposition, though true, may not be a good example of self-evident truth.

Another whole class of truths for which certitude may be claimed consists of those called evident, rather than self-evident. I do not, as Descartes thought, have to infer my existence from the fact that I am aware of myself thinking. I perceive it directly, just as I perceive directly the existence of all the physical objects that surround me. If there is any doubt at all about the truth of such judgments, it is the merest shadow of doubt about whether I am suffering a hallucination rather than actually perceiving.

When I am perceiving, not hallucinating, there can be no doubt that the objects I am perceiving actually exist. Such judgments have a semblance of certitude that falls short of complete certitude only to the extent that a shadow of doubt remains concerning the normality of my perceptual processes.

Whether my perceptual objects exist when I am not perceiving them is another question, to which I think the true answer is that they do, but its truth is neither self-evident nor evident. Reasoning and argument are required to defend its truth. If we go beyond judgments about the present existence of objects that we are at the moment perceiving to judgments about their existence at other times and places, or to judgments about their characteristics or attributes, we pass from the realm of certitude to that of doubt. Though we less frequently misperceive than we misremember, our perceptions as well as our memories give rise to judgments that are often in error or otherwise at fault.

Judgments that articulate what we perceive or remember take the form of statements about particulars—this one thing or that, one event rather than another. We are also prone to generalize on the basis of our perceptual experience. In fact, the judgments we are most likely to be insistent about are generalizations from experience. Many of these are unguarded and turn out to be unwarranted because we have said "all" when we should have said "some." Even scientific generalizations sometimes overstate the case. The history of science contains many examples of generalizations that have been falsified by the discovery of one or more negative instances.

The falsification that I have just referred to provides us with one more example of judgments that belong in the sphere of certitude. When the discovery of a single black swan falsifies the generalization that all swans are white, our judgment that that generalization is false is knowledge in the strong sense of the term—final, infallible, incorrigible. Nothing that might possibly ever happen in the future could reverse the judgment and make it true rather than false that all swans are white.

The number of self-evident truths is very small. The number of falsified generalizations, both those made by scientists and those made by laymen, is considerable; and the number of perceptual judgments about the evident truth of which we have certitude is very large. But it is not the number that matters when we compare the realm of certitude with the realm of doubt. What matters is that only judgments in the realm of doubt have a future, a future in which the effort we expend in the pursuit of truth may bring us closer to it.

CHAPTER 8

The Pursuit of Truth

IN DIFFERENT DISCIPLINES or departments of learning, progress in the pursuit of truth is accomplished in different ways—by the employment of different methods and by resorting to different devices for correcting errors or expanding knowledge. The way in which mathematicians arrive at new and better formulations has little in common with the way in which historians make new findings and revise earlier views of what happened in the past. Different from both are the procedures of the experimental sciences and the data-gathering routines of the social sciences.

Differences aside, the pursuit of truth in all branches of organized knowledge involves (1) the addition of new truths to the body of settled or established truths already achieved, (2) the replacement of less accurate or less comprehensive formulations by better ones, (3) the discovery of errors or inadequacies together with the rectification of judgments found erroneous or otherwise at fault, and (4) the discarding of generalizations—or of hypotheses and theories—that have been falsified by negative instances.

By all such steps, singly or together, the sphere of truths agreed upon enlarges and comes closer to being the whole truth. As the wheat is separated from the chaff, as agreed-upon errors or falsities are eliminated, it also comes closer to being nothing but the truth.

The complete realization of the ideal that is the goal—the whole truth and nothing but the truth—will never be achieved in any stretch of time. The pursuit is endless. It is in the main progressive, though there are periods when no advances are made and even some when impediments to further progress appear at the time to be insuperable. Nevertheless, the pursuit of truth is never so blocked or frustrated that despair impels us to give up the enterprise.

Viewing the pursuit of truth retrospectively, we find that experts who are competent to judge—mathematicians, scientists, historians, each in their own departments of learning—have reached agreement about a host of judgments that they have come to regard as settled or established truths in their respective fields. This does not mean, of course, that all these agreed-upon truths have the finality and incorrigibility of certitude. It means only that the shadow of a doubt that still hangs over them because of what an uncharted future has in store does not at the present moment threaten their status as established truth, temporarily undisputed by experts competent to judge.

Looking toward the future, the ongoing pursuit of truth presents a different picture. On the periphery of the sphere of truth in each department of learning lie disputed matters about which experts are not in agreement. Out of each conflict of opinion emerges the investigations, researches, criticisms, and arguments by which it is hoped the disputes can be resolved and agreement achieved. When that occurs, the matter under dispute becomes a settled matter, and the pursuit of truth pushes the edges of inquiry on to matters still disputable.

The movement from the disputable to things no longer disputed, or from areas of disagreement to things about which agreement has been reached, gives direction to the pursuit of truth. Each step in that direction is a dramatic episode in the long history of mankind's effort to know as much as can be known.

The sphere of truth, in short, is the sphere of those matters about which we think disagreement is profitable precisely because we think these are matters about which it is possible to resolve differences of opinion and to reach agreement instead. There are matters of a quite different sort concerning which we think the very opposite. These are matters of taste rather than of truth.

We are all acquainted with the commonplace maxim *De gustibus non disputandum est.* About matters of taste, there is no point in arguing. Disputes are fruitless. Our differences of opinion look irreconcilable. Arguing about such matters will not bring us into agreement. On the contrary, we should wisely live with and gladly tolerate differences of opinion that express divergent tastes.

About matters of truth, the opposite maxim should rule: *De veritate disputandum est.* About matters of truth, dispute is fruitful. Wherever the truth of our judgments, opinions, or beliefs is a proper concern, we should be prepared to argue with those who disagree with us, with the firm hope that our disagreement can be resolved. Wisdom does not counsel us here to desist from the effort to reach agreement. Disagreement about matters of truth is not, in the final reckoning, to be tolerated.

I am not saying that, where disagreement about a matter of truth is extremely difficult to resolve, we can expect to achieve the agreement we seek within any specified period of time or by any resources available to us at the moment. I am only saying that we should never abandon our effort to reach the agreement we ought to seek in all matters that fall within the sphere of truth rather than the sphere of taste. To give up is to abandon the pursuit of truth.

We may have to live for a long time with disagreements that cannot be easily resolved. That should not cause us to regard them as permanently-tolerable. As long as it is possible for us to carry on, by empirical and rational means, a process of inquiry directed toward resolving a disputed question and reaching agreement about the answer to it (even if that agreement should itself be altered or transformed in the future), our dedication to the pursuit of truth obliges us to proceed in that direction.

We should never rest satisfied with anything less than the agreement of all (about matters concerning which common sense is competent to judge) or of all who are experts (about matters belonging to special departments of knowledge). Unanimous agreement is the appropriate condition of the human mind with regard to anything that is a matter of truth rather than a matter of taste.

To illustrate the difference between matters of truth and matters of taste, let me offer some examples.

There is a spectrum of matters some of which at one extreme clearly belong to the sphere of truth and some of which at the other extreme just as clearly belong to the sphere of taste. Let us first consider the clear cases at either end of the spectrum.

At one extreme, clearly belonging to the sphere of truth, is mathematics and, associated with it, the exact sciences, especially the experimental sciences. Placing these disciplines in the sphere of truth does not mean that at any time there is perfect agreement among all mathematicians or experimental scientists about everything in their fields. But it does mean that, when they do disagree, we expect them to be able to resolve their disagreements by recourse to rational processes employing the methods and techniques of their disciplines.

Not only would we regard an irresolvable disagreement in

their fields as scandalous and intolerable; not only should we expect mathematicians and experimental scientists to be able to resolve whatever disagreements confront them; but we also think that they are morally obligated to sustain their efforts to settle their disputes until they finally succeed in doing so.

At the opposite extreme, clearly belonging to the sphere of taste, are such matters as cuisine, social manners, styles in dress or dance, patterns of family life, and so on. Here we do not expect human beings to overcome their conflicting predilections or preferences, nor do we think they should try to do so.

We do not look for uniformity in these matters. On the contrary, we are fully acquiescent in an irreducible pluralism in all matters of taste. We would regard as monstrous any attempt to impose universal conformity to any one diet or culinary program, any one set of social manners, life-style, or style of dress.

The adoption of one style rather than another is an act of choice springing from emotional predispositions and cultural conditioning. It is determined extrinsically by temperamental inclinations and by environmental circumstances. In contrast, the affirmation of opinions or beliefs as true and the rejection of their opposites as false involve judgments that are determined intrinsically by the substance of the matters being considered and by reference to the probative force of the relevant evidence and the cogency of the applicable reasoning.

In matters of truth, objective considerations play the major role. Ideally, they should operate exclusively, inhibiting even the slightest intrusion of emotional preference or wishful thinking. The ideal may seldom be fully realized in the actual process whereby mathematicians, scientists, and historians attempt to resolve their differences or settle their disputes. It remains the ideal nevertheless and, being so, it enables us to draw a sharp line of demarcation between the sphere of truth and the sphere of taste. On the other side of that line—in the sphere of taste —temperamental inclinations, emotional predilections, cultural attachments predominate, as they should and must because differences in matters of taste do not yield to reason, to argument, to the weight of the evidence.

One further polarity characterizes the two spheres. The sphere of truth is transcultural. Where at a given time it fails to be transcultural, it can become so in the future. The agreement of those who are competent to judge in the fields of mathematics and experimental science transcends all national boundaries as well as the ethnic and cultural barriers that separate different subgroups of mankind.

The sphere of truth is global. To whatever extent the whole human race operates as members of a world community, it is with regard to matters that clearly fall in the sphere of truth rather than in the sphere of taste.

In the sphere of taste, mankind is divided into a multitude of factions and is always likely to remain so. There are those who will always prefer Chinese or Japanese cooking and those who will always prefer the Italian or the French cuisine. This is quite different from the principles of elementary arithmetic, the laws of algebra, the demonstrated theorems of Euclidean geometry, which cannot be characterized by adjectives derived from a nationality or a culture that has produced them. They are not Chinese, Japanese, Italian, French, or anything else like that.

I have been using mathematics on the one hand and styles of cooking or cuisine on the other hand to exemplify as clearly as possible the opposite poles at which lie the sphere of truth and the sphere of taste. Between these polar extremes, philosophical opinions and religious beliefs occupy a middle ground.

The prevalent view today, in academic circles at least, tends to place philosophical opinions and religious belief on the side of taste rather than on the side of truth. That has not always been the regnant view, nor is it necessarily the correct one.

Many philosophers in the past have looked upon themselves, and some in the present regard themselves, as engaged in the pursuit of truth, seriously concerned with efforts to resolve disputed questions by rational means. For them, the adoption of one philosophical position rather than another is not determined by emotional preference or personal prejudice.

What, then, leads one to place philosophy in the middle—

not as clearly in the sphere of truth as mathematics and experimental science, nor as clearly in the sphere of taste as styles of cuisine or dress? The answer lies in an undeniable historical fact. Over the centuries there has been less evident progress in the pursuit of philosophical truth than has been manifest in the advances made in mathematics and experimental science. Also, over the centuries and at a given time, the agreement of philosophers with one another about fundamental matters falls far short of the unanimity achieved by mathematicians and experimental scientists with regard to matters that form the core of settled and established truth in those fields.

Differences in religious belief, considered within the orbit of our Western culture or seen from a global perspective, would appear to be even more irreconcilable and less amenable to resolution by rational means. This fact tends to align them more with differences in matters of taste, where dispute is futile, than with differences in the sphere of truth, where dispute is not only profitable but obligatory.

Nevertheless, adherents of different religious faiths are seldom willing to accept this alignment as correct. Orthodox believers are wont to regard their religious beliefs as constituting the one true faith. The missionary zeal of proselyters springs from the conviction that reason, not merely emotion, is at work in the process of converting the heathens, gentiles, or infidels. It is by opening the mind to the truth, not by coercion or duress, that religious conversion should be consummated.

With regard to the very difficult problem of assessing the position of philosophy and religion on one or the other side of the line that divides the sphere of truth from the sphere of taste, I must content myself with three brief observations.

First, whatever allocation one makes, the determination itself should be regarded as a judgment that is genuinely disputable. It, therefore, belongs in the sphere of truth rather than of taste.

Second, if the judgment is that philosophy and religion are composite in character, combining matters of truth with matters of taste, then, so far as these matters can be separated, they should be dealt with in a manner that is appropriate to the sphere to which they belong.

Third, to whatever extent philosophical opinions and religious beliefs belong to the sphere of truth, we should look upon disputed questions in these fields as resolvable by rational means. However difficult it may be to resolve them, our obligation here, in the pursuit of truth, is to be unrelenting in our efforts to reach agreement—even if it takes until the end of time to do so.

When we recognize that the possession of truth is the ultimate good of the human mind, and, recognizing this, commit ourselves to the pursuit of truth, we have a number of moral obligations to discharge.

About any human judgment (whether made by a person of common sense or made by an expert in one of the learned disciplines) we must ask, Does the judgment belong to the sphere of truth or to the sphere of taste?

Upon deciding that it belongs to the sphere of truth, we should then look for and examine the grounds upon which it may be judged either true or false.

If our own affirmation or denial of its truth brings us into disagreement with others (*either* about whether it properly belongs to the sphere of truth *or* about whether it is true), then we have one further obligation to discharge. We must take whatever steps of inquiry can be employed effectively to resolve such disagreement.

However difficult and protracted that process may be, we must never tire of carrying it on. We must never suspend further inquiry as futile or discontinue argument as profitless. To do so is to abandon the pursuit of truth and to treat the matter in question as if it belonged to the sphere of taste.

Only if we fully discharge all these obligations are we entitled to regard ourselves as engaged in a lifelong commitment to the pursuit of truth.

CHAPTER 9

From Truth to Goodness and Beauty

OF THESE THREE GREAT IDEAS, TRUTH is sovereign as, in the case of the second trio, JUSTICE is the governing idea in relation to liberty and equality.

Matters that we have come to understand better through our consideration of truth—the distinction between judgments having certitude and judgments in the realm of doubt, the distinction between the sphere of truth and the sphere of taste—lay the ground for a better understanding of goodness and beauty.

We have faced the question about the subjective aspect of truth and its relation to the objective aspect; and we have seen why the objective aspect is primary and controlling. This will guide us in dealing with similar questions about goodness and beauty, questions that we will find more insistent and more difficult.

Was the skeptical Montaigne correct when he said that there is nothing good or evil but thinking makes it so? Are people generally right in saying that beauty exists only in the eye of the beholder?

Is there no objective aspect of goodness or beauty? Can some of our judgments about what is good and evil, or about what is right and wrong, be placed in the sphere of truth, leaving others in the sphere of taste? What is the basis for allocating them in this way?

Are the objective and subjective aspects of beauty so inseparably fused that it is impossible, in the case of beauty, to separate what is a matter of truth from what is a matter of taste? Does the maxim *De gustibus non disputandum est* apply without exception to all judgments about goodness and beauty; or do some fall under the maxim *De veritate disputandum est?*

The milder forms of skepticism that I have called subjectivism and relativism are rampant not only in the popular mind but also in academic circles, especially among sociologists and other behaviorial scientists and even among philosophers. I think I have shown how they can be combated with regard to truth. I hope I shall be able to persuade readers that the mistakes of subjectivism and relativism can also be corrected with regard to goodness.

The importance of doing so should be obvious. If all our judgments about good and evil, right and wrong, are purely subjective; if they are simply expressions of emotional preference; if there is no point in resorting to rational argument when we find ourselves in conflict with others about such matters, the practical consequences are far-reaching and pervasive. They impinge upon the conduct of our personal and public lives at every turn.

Subjectivism and relativism with regard to beauty are much less amenable to correction than with regard to goodness. Fortunately, it is also less important to overcome them there, at least so far as their practical effect upon our lives is concerned.

CHAPTER 10

Is and Ought

THE JUDGMENT THAT SOMETHING IS GOOD OR BAD—or that it is better or worse than something else—is one we make every day, often many times a day. It is implicit in every choice we make. It is expressed every time we appraise anything or estimate its value for us. That is why judgments that attribute goodness or some degree of goodness to things have come to be called "value judgments."

We see at once a fundamental difference between truth and goodness. We do not usually speak of things as being true or false. In exceptional cases, such as that of counterfeit money, we may think of the counterfeit as false and of the genuine article as true, but when we do so, we are using the words "true" and "false" in a metaphorical sense, borrowing the words from their proper application to the verbal statements we make or the judgments of our mind.

"Good" and "bad," on the other hand, are terms we normally apply to the things of this world, not to our thoughts or statements about them. Included among the items we appraise as good or bad are human beings themselves, as well as their intentions and actions, their institutions and productions, and the lives they lead. In every case, it is the object we are considering, not our thought about it, that we call good or bad.

Traditional wisdom places the difference between truth and goodness in the different relationships they involve. Truth resides in the relation between the thinking mind and the objects it thinks about. Our thoughts are true when they stand in a relation of agreement with the state of the objects we are thinking about. Goodness resides in the relation between objects of every sort and the state of our desires. Objects are good when they satisfy our desires.

When we talk about the pursuit of truth, we are regarding truth as an object of desire and, in doing so, we are in effect attributing goodness to truth. Having possession of the truth in some measure is a good of the mind, a good we seek when we pursue the truth. If we seek to overcome ignorance and to avoid error, we regard them as evils to be avoided; and in their place, we desire knowledge, which consists in having some hold on the truth about the way things are.

Now let us turn in the opposite direction and ask whether there is any truth in our value judgments—our judgments about things as good or bad. When such judgments are challenged, most people find it difficult to defend them by giving reasons calculated to persuade others to agree with them. Since individuals obviously differ from one another in their desires, what one person regards as good may not be so regarded by another.

Unless I am lying, my statement that I regard something as good (which is tantamount to saying that I desire it) is a true statement about me, but that would seem to be as far as it goes.

The judgment that the object in question is good would not appear to be true in a sense that commands universal assent— good not just for me but for everyone else as well.

We are thus brought face to face with the much disputed question about the objectivity or subjectivity of value judgments. In the contemporary world, skepticism about value judgments prevails on all sides. Value judgments, it is generally thought, express nothing more than individual likes or dislikes, desires or aversions. They are entirely subjective and relative to the individual who makes them. If they have any truth at all, it is only the truth that is contained in a statement about the individual who is making the judgment—the truth that he regards a certain object as good because he, in fact, desires it.

Only if there could be truth in judgments that asserted that certain objects are good for all human beings, not just for this individual or that, would value judgments have objectivity. They would then cease to be entirely relative to individual idiosyncrasies. At least some value judgments would then belong in the sphere of truth and be subject to argument. Others might remain in the sphere of taste and be beyond the reach of argument. We might expect men to try to achieve agreement about the former, but not about the latter. Instead of saying that good and bad are entirely subjective values, we would then be maintaining that they are partly objective and partly subjective.

However, this is precisely what is denied by skepticism concerning value judgments, at least those that appraise objects as good and bad, which is just another way of saying desirable and undesirable. In the skeptic's view, the identification of the good with the desirable makes it impossible to avoid the subjectivity of judgments about what is good and bad, relative as they must be to the differing desires of different individuals.

That the good is the desirable and the desirable is the good cannot be denied. But we can note a certain duplicity in the meaning of "desirable." When we speak of something as desirable, we may mean, on the one hand, that *it is in fact desired* and, on the other hand, that *it ought to be desired*, whether or not it is. Certainly, when we say that something is admirable, we can either be reporting the fact that it *is* admired or be laying down the injunction that it *ought* to be admired, whether or not it is. The same duplicity would seem to be present in the meaning of desirable.

With this duplicity in mind, we can ask the following critical question: Do we regard something as good simply because we in fact desire it, or ought we to desire something because it is in fact good? In both cases, the good remains the desirable, but in one case the goodness is attributed to the object only because it is desired, while in the other the object ought to be desired only because it is good.

The alternatives here presented are not exclusive. We can affirm that some of an individual's value judgments attribute goodness to an object on the basis of the fact that he or she desires it. We can also affirm that some of an individual's value judgments recognize a goodness in the object that makes it an object that ought to be desired.

The skeptical view of value judgments holds that they are all of the same sort. All consist in an individual's calling an object good on the basis of his actual desires. That which he in fact desires appears good to him insofar as he desires it. The object that appears good to him may not appear good to someone else whose desires are different. One man's meat is another man's poison.

Against the skeptic, are we able to defend the opposite view that, while some objects appear good to an individual simply because he or she in fact desires them, there are other objects that he or she ought to desire because they are good—really good, not just apparently good?

To do this, we must manage to get across another hurdle. The obstacle that now stands in our way is a difficulty that has been raised about prescriptive as opposed to descriptive statements.

A prescriptive statement or judgment is one that asserts what ought or ought not to be done. A statement about what ought or ought not to be desired imposes a prescription that may or may not be obeyed. In contradistinction, a descriptive statement or judgment is one that asserts the way things are, not how they ought to be. A statement about what is desired by a given individual simply describes his condition as a matter of fact.

How, it is asked, can prescriptive injunctions be true or false? Have we not adopted the view that the truth of statements or judgments consists in their conformity with the ways things are—with the facts that they try to describe? If a statement is true when it asserts that that which is, is, and false when it asserts that which is, is not, how then can there be truth or falsity in a statement that asserts what ought or ought not to be?

Even if we possessed all the descriptive truth that is attainable, how could our knowledge of reality, our knowledge of the way things are, lead us to any valid conclusion about what ought to be done or about what ought to be desired?

It was long ago quite correctly pointed out by the skeptical philosopher David Hume that no prescriptive conclusion (in the form of an "ought" statement) can be validly inferred from a set of premises, no matter how complete, that consists solely of descriptive statements about the way things are. Even if we had perfect knowledge of all the properties that enter into the description of an object, we could not infer the goodness of the object or that it ought to be desired.

We are thus confronted with two obstacles, not one. The first is the difficulty raised by the question, How can prescriptive statements be either true or false, if truth consists in the correspondence between what is asserted and the way things are? The second is the objection raised by David Hume, to the effect that truths about matters of fact do not enable us to reach by reasoning a single valid prescriptive conclusion—a true judgment about what ought or ought not to be done or desired.

Unless we can surmount these difficulties, no prescriptive statement or judgment can be true or false. If we cannot truly say what ought to be desired, then the good is the desirable only in the sense that it appears good to the individual who in fact desires it. Acquiescing in the rejection of the alternative sense of the desirable as that which ought to be desired, we also must give up the notion that some objects are really good as distinguished from other objects that only appear to be good and may not be really so.

To refute the skeptical view, which makes all value judgments subjective and relative to individual desires, we must be able to show how prescriptive statements can be objectively true. An understanding of truth as including more than the kind of truth that can be found in descriptive statements thus becomes the turning point in our attempt to establish a certain measure of objectivity in our judgments about what is good and bad.

Only through such understanding will we be able to show that some value judgments belong to the sphere of truth, instead of all being relegated to the sphere of taste and thus reduced to matters about which reasonable men should not argue with one another or expect to reach agreement.

CHAPTER 11

Real and Apparent Goods

SKEPTICISM WITH REGARD TO TRUTH reared its head in antiquity. Confronted with it, the ancients came up with its refutation. Not so with regard to goodness.

Skepticism about value judgments—about the validity of our attribution of goodness to objects and about the truth of any statement that contains the words "ought" or "ought not"— begins in the modern world. Without having been confronted with that brand of skepticism, the ancients provided us with clues enabling us to separate that aspect of the good that has the objectivity of truth from that aspect that is entirely subjective and relative to the individual.

At the dawn of modern thought, Thomas Hobbes and Benedict Spinoza advanced the view that "good" was merely the name we gave to those things that in fact we happened to desire or like. Goodness is not a discoverable property of the things themselves. We simply call them good because we desire them. If we had an aversion to them instead, we would call them bad.

Since desires and aversions are matters of individual temperament, nurture, and predilection, there is nothing that all human beings agree upon as deserving to be called good or bad. Just as the skeptic concerning truth says that what is true for me may not be true for you, so here the skeptic says that what is good for you may not be good for me.

A century or more later, David Hume, as we have seen, added another arrow to the quiver of skepticism about values. He pointed out that from our knowledge of the facts about nature or reality (as complete as one might wish it to be), we cannot validate a single value judgment that ascribes to the object a goodness that makes it true to say that all men ought to desire it. Those who, before or after Hume, identify the good with pleasure or the pleasing, do not avoid the thrust of his skeptical challenge. Rather, they reinforce it, for what pleases one individual may not please another; and, in any case, the goodness that is identified with pleasure does not reside in the object but in the emotional experience of the individual.

Hume's challenge is further reinforced in our own century by a group of thinkers whose names are associated with a doctrine that has come to be called "noncognitive ethics." They use the word "ethics" to refer to the whole sphere of moral judgments about good and bad, or right and wrong, especially in the form of prescriptions about what ought and ought not to be sought or what ought and ought not to be done. Their dismissal of ethics as "noncognitive" is their way of saying that statements that assert an ought or an ought-not cannot be either true or false.

Not capable of being either true or false, such assertions are noncognitive. They do not belong to the sphere of knowledge, even in the weaker sense of that term, which connotes verifiable or supportable opinion. Thrown out of the sphere of truth, they are relegated to the sphere of taste. They are at best expressions of personal predilection or prejudice, entirely relative to the feelings, impulses, whims, or wishes of the individual.

If we ask why judgments about what ought to be desired or done are totally incapable of being either true or false, the answer appeals to an understanding of what truth and falsity consist in—an understanding first formulated in antiquity and one that these twentieth-century exponents of a noncognitive ethics adopt. Once we conceive the truth of a statement as residing in its correspondence with the facts of the matter under consideration, with the way things really are, we are led to the conclusion that only statements that assert that something is or is not the case can be either true or false—true if they assert that which is in fact the way things are, false if they assert the opposite.

All such statements can be characterized as descriptions of reality. Statements that contain the words "ought" or "ought not" are prescriptions or injunctions, not descriptions of anything. If our understanding of truth and falsity conceives them as properties that can be found only in descriptions, then we cannot avoid the skeptical conclusion that prescriptive statements cannot be either true or false.

A moment's reflection will lead us to see that the only way that this skeptical conclusion can be avoided is by expanding our understanding of truth. Can we find another mode of truth, one that is appropriate to prescriptions or injunctions, just as the more familiar mode of truth is appropriate to descriptions, or statements of fact? How can oughts and ought-nots be true?

For the answer to this question, we must go back to antiquity —to the thought of Plato and Aristotle. Aristotle, following Plato, formulated the conception of truth that has been generally adopted in Western thought—the one that is appealed to by the exponents of noncognitive ethics when they maintain that only descriptive statements can be either true or false. However, he did not stop there. Recognizing that that mode of truth did not apply to prescriptive statements or injunctions (which he called "practical" because they are regulative of human action), he proposed another mode of truth appropriate to practical judgments.

That mode of truth, he said, consists in the conformity of such judgments with right desire, as the other mode of truth consists in the correspondence of our descriptions of reality with the reality that they claim to describe.

Unfortunately, Aristotle did not explain what he meant by right desire. We are, therefore, on our own in pushing the inquiry farther.

What is right desire? It would appear that the answer must be that right desire consists in desiring what we ought to desire, as wrong desire consists in desiring what we ought not to desire.

What ought one to desire? The answer cannot be—simply and without qualification—that we ought to desire what is good. We have already seen that the good is always and only the desirable and the desirable is always and only the good. As Plato's Socrates repeatedly pointed out, we never desire anything that we do not, at the moment of desiring it, deem to be good. Hence we must somehow find a way of distinguishing between the goods that we rightly desire and the goods that we wrongly desire.

We are helped to do this by the distinction that Socrates makes between the real and the apparent good. He repeatedly reminds us that our regarding something as good because we in fact desire it does not make it really good in fact. It may, and often does, turn out to be the very opposite. What appears to be good at the time we desire it may prove to be bad for us at some later time or in the long run. The fact that we happen to desire something may make it appear good to us at the time, but it does not make it really good for us.

If the good were always and only that which appears good to us because we consciously desire it, it would be impossible to distinguish between right and wrong desire. Aristotle's conception of practical or prescriptive truth would then become null and void. It can be given content only if we can distinguish between the apparent good (that which we call good simply because we consciously desire it at a given moment) and the real good (that which we ought to desire whether we do in fact desire it or not).

Up to this point we seem to be running around in circles. We have identified the real good with that which we ought to desire. We have interpreted right desire as consisting in desiring what one ought to desire, which amounts to saying that it consists in desiring what is really good. To say that the truth of a prescriptive or practical judgment, which tells us what we ought to desire, consists in conformity with right desire amounts to saying that a prescription is true if it tells us that we ought to desire what we ought to desire. And that is saying nothing at all.

The only way to get out of this circle is to find some way of identifying what is really good for us that does not equate it merely with what we ought to desire. How can that be done? Aristotle provides us with the answer by calling our attention to a fundamental distinction in the realm of desire.

On the one hand, there are the desires inherent in our human nature, rooted in potentialities or capacities that drive or tend toward fulfillment. These are our natural desires, desires with which we are innately endowed. Because they are inherent in human nature, as all truly specific properties are, they are present in all human beings, just as human facial characteristics, human skeletal structure, or human blood types are. Not only are they present in all human beings, as inherent properties of human nature, but they are always operative tendentially or appetitively (that is, they always tend toward or seek fulfillment), whether or not at a given moment we are conscious of such tendencies or drives.

On the other hand, there are the desires that each individual acquires in the course of his or her life, each as the result of his or her own individual experience, conditioned by his or her individual temperament and by the circumstances of his or her individual life. Consequently, unlike natural desires, which are the same in all human beings, acquired desires differ from individual to individual, as individuals differ in their temperaments, experiences, and the circumstances of their lives. Also, unlike our natural desires, of which we may not be conscious at a given moment, we are always conscious of our acquired desires at the time they are motivating us in one direction or another.

The quickest and easiest way to become aware of the validity of this distinction between natural and acquired desires is to employ two words that are in everyone's vocabulary and are in daily use. Let us use the word "needs" for our natural desires, and the word "wants" for the desires we acquire. Translated into these familiar terms, what we have said so far boils down to this: that all human beings have the same specifically human needs, whereas individuals differ from one another with regard to the things they want.

The use of the words "need" and "want" enables us to go further. Our common understanding of needs provides us at once with the insight that there are no wrong or misguided needs. That is just another way of saying that we never need anything that is really bad for us—something we ought to avoid. We recognize that we can have wrong or misguided wants. That which we want may appear to be good to us at the time, but it may not be really good for us. Our needs are never excessive, as our wants often are. We can want too much of a good thing, but we can never need too much of whatever it is we need. We can certainly want more than we need.

One thing more, and most important of all: We cannot ever say that we ought or ought not to need something. The words "ought" and "ought not" apply only to wants, never to needs. This means that the natural desires that are our inborn needs enter into the sphere of our voluntary conduct only through the operation of our acquired desires or wants. In other words, we may or may not in fact want what we need. Almost all of us want things that we do not need and fail to want things that we do need.

In the statement just made lies the crux of the matter. We ought to want the things we need. We ought not to want the things we do not need if wanting them interferes with our wanting—and acquiring—the things we do need.

The distinction between needs and wants enables us to draw the line between real goods and apparent goods. Those things that satisfy or fulfill our needs or natural desires are things that are really good for us. Those that satisfy our wants or acquired desires are things that appear good to us when we consciously desire them. If we need them as well as want them, they are also really good for us.

However, if we only want them and do not need them, they will nevertheless appear good to us because we want them. Beyond that, they may either turn out to be harmless or innocuous (in that they do not impede or prevent our acquiring the real goods we need) or they may turn out to be the very opposite (quite harmful or really bad for us because they somehow deprive us of one or another of the real goods we need).

We cannot ever be mistaken about our wants. No one can be incorrect in saying that he wants something. But it is quite possible for individuals to be mistaken about their needs. Children are frequently given to thinking or saying that they need something when they should have said that they want it. Adults are prone to making the same mistake.

If we can be mistaken about our needs, does not that weaken the underpinning of our argument so far? To avoid this, we must be able to determine with substantial accuracy the needs inherent in human nature. Since their gratification often requires the presence of certain favorable environmental circumstances, we must also be able to determine the indispensable external conditions that function instrumentally in the satisfaction of needs (e.g., a healthy environment is instrumentally needed to safeguard the health of its members).

Success in these efforts depends on the adequacy of our knowledge and understanding of human nature in itself and in its relation to the environment.

It is by reference to our common human needs that we claim to know what is really good for all human beings. Knowing this, we are also justified in claiming that we can determine the truth or falsity of prescriptions or injunctions. As Aristotle said, prescriptions are true if they conform to right desire.

All our needs are right desires because those things that satisfy our natural desires are things that are really good for us. When we want what we need, our wants are also right desires.

The injunction to want knowledge, for example, is a true prescription—the true statement of an ought—because human beings all need knowledge. As Aristotle pointed out, man by nature desires to know. Since the acquired desire for knowledge is a right desire, because it consists in wanting what everyone needs, the prescription "You ought to want and seek knowledge" is universally and objectively true—true for all human beings—because it conforms to a right desire that is rooted in a natural need.

No one, I think, would question man's need for knowledge or the truth of the prescription that everyone ought to want and seek knowledge. That truth comes to us as the conclusion of reasoning that rests on two premises.

The first is a categorical prescription or injunction: We ought to desire (seek and acquire) that which is really good for us.

The second is a statement of fact about human nature: Man has a potentiality or capacity for knowing that tends toward or seeks fulfillment through the acquirement of knowledge. In other words, the facts about human nature are such that, if we are correct in our grasp of them, we can say that man needs knowledge and that knowledge is really good for man.

Now, if the foregoing categorical prescription or injunction is true and if in addition the foregoing statement of fact about human nature's involving a need for knowledge is true, then the prescriptive conclusion, that everyone ought to want and seek knowledge, not only follows from the premises, but is also true—true by conforming to right desire as set forth in the categorical prescription that we ought to want and seek that which is really good for us (i.e., that which by nature we need).

The truth of the categorical prescription that underlies every piece of reasoning that leads to a true prescriptive conclusion is a self-evident truth. Anyone can test this for himself by trying to think the opposite and finding it impossible.

We simply cannot think that we ought to desire that which is really bad for us or that we ought not to desire that which is really good for us. Without knowing in advance which things are in fact really good or bad for us, we do know at once that "ought to desire" is inseparable in its meaning from the meaning of "really good," just as we know at once that the parts of a physical whole are always less than the whole. It is impossible to think the opposite just as it is impossible to think that we ought to desire that which is really bad for us.

We acknowledge a truth as self-evident as soon as we acknowledge the impossibility of thinking the opposite.

What about the truth of the other premise in the reasoning? That is a factual premise. It asserts a fact about human nature. As I pointed out a little earlier, Aristotle's observation that man by nature desires to know seems unquestionable. Man's natural desire or need for knowledge being acknowledged, the factual premise can be asserted as true—if not with certitude, then with a very high degree of assurance. It is beyond a reasonable doubt if not beyond the shadow of a doubt. That suffices for present purposes.

What about other natural desires or needs, about which we must make accurate statements of fact if we are to proceed with reasoning that will yield us other true prescriptive conclusions?

I have already admitted that, while we can never make a misstatement about our wants, we may be mistaken about our needs, declaring that we need something that we should have said we wanted, or failing to recognize that we need something that we do not want. Such mistakes would result in false rather than true factual assertions about human nature and the desires that are inherent in it.

The consequence of this is obvious. The prescriptive conclusions to which our practical reasoning would lead us would then be false rather than true, practically or prescriptively false because the errors we have made about matters of fact prevent the conclusions from conforming to right desire.

Therefore, what remains for further inquiry is whether our knowledge of human nature enables us to identify—with sufficient assurance, not with certitude—the real goods that fulfill man's natural desires or needs. I will undertake to approximate this in the following chapter, concerned with the range and scale of goods.

To complete our picture of the matters covered in this chapter, one closing comment must be added. I conceded earlier that David Hume was correct in pointing out that from our knowledge of matters of fact about reality or real existence, *and from that alone,* we cannot validly reason to a true prescriptive conclusion—a judgment about what one ought or ought not to desire or do.

In the foregoing statement, I have italicized the words "and from that alone." Upon that qualification, the correctness of Hume's point rests. It follows, therefore, that practical or prescriptive reasoning can be validly carried on if it does not rely upon factual knowledge alone.

The reasoning to be found in the preceding pages of this chapter relies on factual knowledge but not on that alone. Factual knowledge is represented solely in the second or minor premise—the one that asserts a certain fact about human nature; for example, that man by nature desires to know. The prescriptive conclusion, that everyone ought to want and seek knowledge, does not rest on that premise alone. It rests on that premise combined with the first and major premise—a categorical prescription that is self-evidently true, the injunction that we ought to want and seek whatever is really good for us.

Upon this one categorical prescription rest all the prescriptive truths we can validate concerning the real goods that we ought to seek, limited only by the extent to which we can discover, with reasonable assurance, the facts about human nature and its inherent desires or needs.

CHAPTER 12

The Range and Scale of Goods

ALL THE GOODS THAT FULFILL OUR NEEDS or satisfy our wants belong in the category of human goods, real or apparent. These are things that are good *for* man.

When we use the word "good" substantively to call them "goods," we are using the word in its primary connotation to signify objects of desire. The goods thus named are diverse embodiments of goodness, the idea of which identifies the good with the desirable.

Not all the things we call good fall into this category; not all are in one way or another objects of human desire. The adjective "good" has a much wider range of meanings than the notion of goodness that we express when we use the word "good" as a noun to designate this or that particular good to be desired.

"Good," like many other adjectives, enables us to express three degrees of evaluation—the positive, the comparative, and the superlative ("good," "better," "best"). But we use "good" more than any other adjective for the purpose of ranking or grading things.

The judges who award bronze, silver, and gold medals at athletic contests are engaged in ranking the performances of the athletes, and are, in effect, saying of these performances "good," "better," "best." The same thing is true of the judges who hand out ribbons of various colors at flower shows, dog shows, or cattle shows.

It is true also of the professional experts who grade coffee beans, wines, and other products bought and sold in the marketplace. In these cases, as in the international ranking of chess and tennis players, the gradations exceed the three expressed by "good," "better," and "best," but there will always be one that is ranked as supremely good, and, with regard to the rest, one will be ranked as superior to another until one comes to the very bottom of the scale.

We have by no means exhausted the extraordinary diversity of things to which we apply the adjective "good" or its higher degrees of "better" and "best." We speak of a good time and of one occasion as being a better time than another, of good weather and of one climate as better than another. We speak of something as good-looking and of something else as better-looking. There are good and bad reasons, better and worse reasons; good and bad intentions, better and worse intentions. One individual, we may say, has a good memory or a good appetite, and another a better memory or appetite.

The things we rank or grade in this way may be judged for their usefulness or for the pleasure they afford us; or they may simply be judged for their intrinsic worth as having the excellence appropriate to that kind of thing. Thus "good," "better," and "best" may mean more or less useful, more or less pleasant, more or less excellent.

Another set of adjectives is available to us for the purpose of grading or ranking things. We can substitute "fine," "finer,"

and "finest" for "good," "better," and "best." Making this substitution would help us to avoid a use of the word "good" that
does not express the judgment that the thing in question has a
goodness that is good *for* us, either because we do in fact desire
it or because it is something that we ought to desire.

All the things we have enumerated as things that can be
graded or ranked with regard to their usefulness, their pleasant-
ness, or their intrinsic worth or excellence may of course also
be judged by someone to be desirable. Then, of course, it becomes a good *for* him or her. The ranking or grading that was
done by someone else, without any explicit reference to desire
on his or her part, does by implication at least involve a reference to desirability.

One object ranked as better than another is preferable or
more desirable than another. The object ranked as best is most
desirable—preferable to all others. Yet a given individual may
not in fact desire the better or the best, and so it is not even a
good for him, real or apparent.

It is interesting to observe that the adjective "true" does not
work in the same way as "good." There are no degrees of objective truth. A statement is either true or false; one statement
is not "truer" than another. We may have more or less assurance in claiming that a certain statement is true, but the degree
of our assurance does not make the statement more or less true.

An elaborate scientific theory or a complex philosophical doctrine may be said to have more truth in it than some other
which it is offered to replace. But whatever amount of truth it
has consists in the number of elements it contains that are true;
the truth of these is not subject to degree.

Now let us return to the primary connotation of the word
"good" as the name for the desirable thing itself—goods that
one wants or needs, all of them goods for man. Confining ourselves for the moment to real goods, we use the word in its
primary meaning when we speak of each of the following as a
particular kind of good: wealth, health, pleasure, friends or

loved ones, liberty or freedom of action, and knowledge and skill in all their forms.

The division of the goods for man into real and apparent goods is far from being the only subdivision within that category. We can see this at once if we turn to goods that are subjects of daily conversation—the goods of the marketplace, the so-called economic goods in the production and exchange of which all our commerce and industry is engaged and toward the acquirement of which we work in our effort to earn a living or secure a livelihood.

We are all aware that there is a vast plurality and a striking diversity of such goods. When, in the economic sphere, we speak of goods and services, we use the word "goods" in a restricted sense to designate only purchasable commodities that have been produced for sale. Hirable services are also purchasable. Since we seek to obtain by purchase the things we need or want, services no less than commodities are economic goods.

Among such goods, economists tell us, some have value in use, some have value in exchange; some are consumable goods, some are instruments or means of production; and one, money, in the form of coin or paper, is solely a medium of exchange— a means of purchasing commodities and services, or instruments of production.

This whole set of goods constitutes the category of goods we call wealth. Within that category, we can distinguish the goods that are merely or solely means and the goods that are ends as well as means. Money is obviously nothing but a means. Except for the pathological deviant who is a miser or the equally misguided figure of King Midas with his lust for gold, no one desires money for its own sake. It fulfills no natural need. To want it for its own sake, as Midas did, is to end up starving, deprived of the real goods that money can and should buy.

Capital goods—instruments of production—are also mere means, desired for the sake of the consumable goods they can produce. The individual who sought to accumulate only capital goods would be as misguided as Midas or the miser and end up as deprived—bereft of friends, naked, unsheltered, and starving to death.

Money, used not as a medium of exchange but as financial capital to be invested or loaned, and physical capital used as instruments of production provide sources of income that confer purchasing power for buying consumable commodities and for hiring useful services. Thus used, they still remain means, and mere means at that.

Among economic goods, the only form of wealth that is not a mere means consists in consumable goods, including here services as well as commodities. Some of these fulfill certain of our biological needs (our needs for food, drink, clothing, shelter, and so on), and some satisfy our individual wants.

While consumable goods are not mere means, neither are they goods that we desire for their own sake and that alone. We need them for the sake of our bodily health, or we want them as conditions prerequisite to activities in which we wish to engage. Like those consumable goods that fulfill our biological needs, physical health (together with bodily vigor and vitality) is also a real good, but a real good that is desired for its own sake as well as for the sake of other goods, to the achievement of which it is a prerequisite condition.

The good, real or apparent, can also be divided into the good we desire to *have*, the good we desire to *do*, and the good we desire to *be*.

1. The good we desire to *have* can be further subdivided into possessions or perfections, and into goods of choice and goods of chance. Wealth exemplifies a possession; health a perfection. Each, as we shall see, is in part at least a good of chance. Only such perfections as good habits and knowledge are entirely goods of choice.

All possessions are external goods—goods that exist apart from the individual who desires to possess them. In addition to wealth, the category of external goods includes friends or loved ones and also all the external circumstances of the individual's life that flow from the institutions and arrangements of the society in which he lives.

As distinguished from possessions, perfections are internal goods—internal in the sense that they have their existence in the person rather than apart from him or her. As used here, the word "perfection" has a restricted connotation. It means only that which completes or fulfills a potentiality of the human being—a capacity for development of one sort or another. In this sense, health is a personal perfection, the pleasures of sense and aesthetic pleasures are personal perfections, and so are all forms of knowledge and skill.

The goods of choice are those which we are able to attain entirely by activities in which we voluntarily engage. If, for example, certain habits are good not only in themselves, but also as means to a good life, we can achieve these perfections through actions entirely within our own power to perform, if we choose to do so. It would appear to be the case that, like knowledge, skill, and other good habits, all goods of choice are internal goods—perfections of the person.

All external goods are goods of chance. While the possession of them may in part depend upon actions that we voluntarily perform according to the choices we make, they never depend solely on what we ourselves choose to do. They are all circumstantial goods in the sense that our possession of them depends either partly or wholly on circumstances beyond our control. In that sense, they are goods of chance, conferred on us by what we call "good luck" or "good fortune," and withheld from us by the misfortunes that befall us.

The goods we desire to *have* may be either real or apparent goods, real if they are personal perfections we ought to seek, such as health, good habits, or knowledge; apparent if they are possessions we want but do not need. In contrast, the other two—the goodness that resides in our doing or action and the goodness that belongs to our being—fall wholly on the side of real goods we ought to desire.

2. The good we should desire to *do* is either an action on our

part that is good for us because it results in our acquirement of an external possession or a personal perfection that we need; or it is an action that results in a real good for someone else, benefiting that other individual or at least not causing injury. As affecting the welfare of others, we usually speak of an individual's actions as right and wrong, or just and unjust.

As we shall see when we come to the consideration of justice, the notions of right and wrong, in the sphere of conduct that impinges on the welfare and well-being of others, are subsidiary to the notions of good and evil. If we did not first know what was really good for any human being, we could not appraise actions as right and wrong—as resulting in benefits or injuries.

3. The good we should desire to *be* is the excellence of a good man or woman. A good man or woman is one who has achieved the personal perfections that fulfill his or her potentialities or capacities for being human. Preeminent among these perfections is the acquired habit of desiring what one ought to desire and desiring nothing that interferes with obtaining the real goods one needs to lead a good life. While, as we shall see, a good man or woman is one who acts justly toward others, good deeds alone do not make a good human being. That is only one element in leading a good life.

A good life is made by accumulating in the course of a lifetime everything that is really good and by wanting nothing that impedes or frustrates this effort. That which appears good to individuals who are good men and women is really good, for they are habitually disposed to want what they ought to want, and not to want what they ought not to.

However, being a good person does not by itself suffice for the achievement of a good human life. Some of the real goods a person needs, especially those that are external or circumstantial goods, are goods of chance. Even the attainment of certain interior perfections are partly dependent upon benign external circumstances.

That is where the benefactions of a good society come in, providing the necessary conditions for a good life that the good person cannot achieve entirely by the choices he or she makes. An organized community is good to the extent that its institutions and arrangements confer upon its members the real goods that everyone needs but which, in whole or part, depend upon external circumstances beyond the individual's control.

A good human being, a good human life, a good society. How are these three principal forms of goodness related to one another?

It would appear that a good society is an external and instrumental good, one that the individual needs to aid and abet his or her effort to make a good life for himself or herself. It would also appear that having the intrinsic virtue or excellence of a good human being is indispensable to achieving a good life.

Why this is so will become clearer presently. For the moment, suffice it to say that a good human life is the ultimate good toward the attainment of which all other goods are instrumental. But it is not the highest good in the hierarchy or scale of particular goods.

At the lowest end of the scale stand the goods that are mere means—goods that ought never to be desired for their own sake but always for the sake of some other good. They are good only to the extent that they are used to obtain goods that fulfill or satisfy other desires.

In the next rung above, we find goods that not only have the character of ends, in that they fulfill or satisfy certain desires, but also serve as means insofar as they are put to use in trying to achieve still other goods. Such goods, desired both for their own sake and for the sake of other goods, fall below the goods they are used to achieve. Wealth and health typify this level of goods.

The highest grade in the whole scale of particular goods consists of those goods that are desired for their own sake and not as means to obtain other particular goods. Enjoyable pleasure is such a good; so also is wisdom. If in the range of particular goods, there is a single highest good (traditionally called the *summum bonum*), it falls here.

It will be noted that at the lowest level of the scale, we find only external goods. At the next level, we find both possessions, such as wealth, and personal perfections, such as health. At the highest level, we find only personal perfections, no possessions or external goods.

There is one further good—one that cannot be included in the scale of goods that we have so far considered because it encompasses the whole scale itself.

All the goods we have so far considered are particular goods. Each is a partial good, one good among others, not the whole constituted by the presence of all the goods needed to make a whole life good. That whole can only be achieved successively and piecemeal in the course of a lifetime; all the particular or partial goods that contribute to this result are constitutive means for achieving the whole.

Even enjoyable pleasure and wisdom among the highest of the particular goods are less than the whole of goods. Though each is desired for its own sake and not for the sake of any other particular good, it does not by itself suffice to satisfy all desires. In addition to being desired for itself, it is desired for the sake of a good life—that whole of which all real goods and some innocuous apparent goods are component parts.

There is still another hierarchy or scale of goodness, one that belongs in the realm of the good to *be* rather than the good to *have* or the good to *do*. Here we are confronted with gradations of goodness that are commensurate with grades of being or existence itself.

Only absolute nonbeing is absolutely evil. Whatever exists to any degree of perfection has a grade of goodness comparable to the perfection of its being or existence. Accordingly, when God is thought of as the Supreme Being, having an infinite existence that lacks no perfection, God is also thought of as supremely good in the scale of beings. This leaves quite open the question about the moral goodness of God—the benevolence, justice, and mercy of the Deity.

St. Augustine's comparison of the goodness of a mouse and of a pearl helps us to understand the goodness commensurate with being. If asked, "Which would you prefer to have?" Augustine thinks the answer should be a pearl, for it is a more valuable possession than a mouse. That is certainly true of its exchange value, and it is likely to be true of its use value and its enjoyability. However, if asked, "Which would you rather be?" he thinks the opposite answer should be given, for a living organism has more being, more potentialities for development, more power to act, than an inert stone, however attractively coated.

As we have seen, the goods we desire to have are either possessions (i.e., external goods) or perfections (i.e., personal goods). The latter increase or amplify our very being through actualizing our potentialities. The man or woman who has become a good human being through acquiring the personal perfections that everyone should desire to have is also the good man or woman that everyone should desire to be. The reason for preferring to be a mouse rather than a pearl is also the reason for preferring to be a good rather than a bad human being.

CHAPTER 13

The Ultimate and Common Good

FOR SOMETHING TO BE ULTIMATE in any dimension or direction, it must be that beyond which one cannot go. What can possibly occupy that unique place in the realm of goods?

We have observed that some goods are mere means, never desired for their own sake, but only for the sake of something else. Other goods, we have noted, are ends as well as means. They are desired for their own sake as well as for the sake of something else. Is there anything that either is or ought to be desired for its own sake and never for the sake of anything else? If so, that is the ultimate good, not just *an* end, but *the* end, the final end beyond which one cannot go.

In antiquity, the word "happiness" was used as the name of this ultimate good. The ancients paid attention to the obvious fact that according to everyone's sense of what the word "happiness" means, it names something desired for its own sake and not for the sake of anything else. It is impossible for anyone to complete the sentence "I want happiness because . . ." except by saying, "I want it." Of anything else that one wants, it is always possible to say, "I want it because it will contribute to my happiness."

The ancients also observed that, while everyone uses the word "happiness" to name that which is desirable solely for itself and not as a means to anything else, individuals differ in their conception of what happiness consists in. If, for the moment, we put aside our basic distinction between real and apparent goods, there will be as many different conceptions of happiness as there are differences with respect to the apparent goods that different individuals want. Each is purely subjective, entirely relative to that individual's wants.

The miser who wants only money, or King Midas who wants everything that he touches turned into gold, should accordingly count himself happy when he gets what he wants. If he wants money or gold for its own sake and if he wants nothing else, he has achieved his goal. He has reached the end of his striving. He has arrived at his ultimate good—his happiness. The same thing can be said of the individual who identifies his happiness with the enjoyment of sensual pleasures, or of the individual who identifies it with gaining and holding power over others.

Once we come back to the distinction between real and apparent goods, the picture changes radically. Far from achieving happiness, the miser, the playboy, and the power-hungry individual have achieved only a counterfeit of it. They have got what they wanted, but not what they ought to want. On the contrary, getting what they want may have resulted in their being deprived of many things they need and ought to want— health, friendships, knowledge, and other goods of the mind.

Properly conceived (which means objectively rather than subjectively conceived), happiness consists in having obtained all the goods that everyone ought to want. So conceived, it is the same for all human beings. It is the common good as well as the ultimate good. It is the ultimate good because it leaves nothing more to be desired, as it would if it were just one particular good among others.

While life goes on, the pursuit of happiness can be defeated by misfortunes of all sorts, or by mistaken choices on the part of the individual. That is why the ancients placed happiness in a whole life well lived—well lived as a result of the individual's choosing as he ought for the most part and also as a result of the individual's being blessed by fortunate external circumstances, again for the most part.

Happiness, we now see, is a human life fulfilled by the accumulation of all the real goods that everyone needs. It is, in addition, a life enriched by whatever apparent goods may be innocuously sought by this or that individual according to his or her different tastes or wants. To confirm this understanding of happiness, we must observe a number of negative strictures.

The first has already been indicated. Happiness is not the supreme good, the *summum bonum,* the highest or best among the real goods to be sought. Instead, it is the totality of goods, the *totum bonum,* the all-inclusive or -encompassing whole comprised of all the real goods. In this sense, it is not *a* good, but *the* good, in the same sense that the ultimate good is not *an* end, but *the* end.

The second negative concerns the character of happiness as *the* end. We usually think of an end as a terminal goal or objective that can be reached and at which, when reached, we come to rest. The end of one's travels lies at the destination where one's traveling terminates, where one stops moving and settles down. The same holds for all other strivings that come to an end when they attain what they are reaching for—all except the striving for happiness.

Conceived as a whole life well lived, happiness is different from all other ends that we strive for or pursue. It is not a terminal goal that can be reached and rested in, for there is no moment of time in which a whole life well lived exists to be enjoyed or experienced. Every other end can be attained at some time during the course of one's life and, as attained, its goodness can be enjoyed or experienced. But the ultimate good that is *the* end cannot be attained short of a whole life being lived.

A whole life comes into existence only with the passage of time. It does not exist at any interval or moment during the time it is coming to be. When we aim at happiness as our ultimate good, we are aiming at something we can never enjoy or experience, as we can the goals that are terminal ends.

If the natural process of human life on earth has a terminal end, it is death, not happiness. Only if there is the hereafter for which religion holds out hope can there be a truly terminal end as the ultimate good and goal of all human striving—the heavenly rest that is enjoyed by the saints in the presence of God. It is certainly understandable why those who yearn and strive for the eternal happiness that is for them the supernatural ultimate good regard as a pale and feeble imitation of it the temporal happiness that is the ultimate good of this earthly life.

The third negative adds a qualification to an earlier statement that happiness as the ultimate good of human life is the same for all human beings. That remains true to the extent that happiness consists in a life fulfilled by the accumulation of all the things that are really good for everyone. But it must also be said that, in another respect, the happiness of one individual is not the same as the happiness of another. Each, according to his individual temperament, nurture, and circumstances, may want quite different things. Consequently, the enrichment of the individual life by the addition of those apparent goods that are innocuous will produce a good life that is somewhat different in its content for one individual and another.

The fourth and final negative calls attention to the fact that happiness is not the same for all in still another respect. Happiness as the ultimate good—the goal at which everyone should aim and toward which everyone should strive—is an ideal that is seldom if ever completely realized.

A terminal goal that we could not reach would be an illusory will-of-the-wisp at the end of the rainbow. Because it is not a terminal end, happiness is not an illusory goal, even though we can achieve it only in some measure or degree that falls short of completeness or perfection. In this respect, one individual may be more successful than another in the pursuit of happiness, either through his own good choices and efforts or through being facilitated in those efforts by the benefactions of good fortune. Accordingly, one individual may achieve a greater measure of happiness than another.

One question remains. We understand that temporal happiness, being a whole life well lived, cannot be a terminal end— a goal that can be reached, enjoyed, and rested in. How, then, can it be an end at all, much less *the* ultimate goal of all our striving?

The answer lies in a function that is performed by any end, whether it is terminal or not. Given an end to be sought or pursued, we are under an obligation to employ whatever means are called for to achieve it, preferring of course the most efficacious of the means available. If we wish to achieve the end in view, we must make use of such and such means.

The imperative here expressed is hypothetical. We must or ought to employ certain means *if*—and *only* if—we desire the end they serve, the goal they can help us to reach. A categorical, not a hypothetical, obligation is imposed on us by happiness as an end or goal. We do not say, "If we wish to achieve a good life, we ought to do this or that." On the contrary, we acknowledge that we ought to aim at a good life, consisting as it does in the attainment of everything really good. This acknowledgment follows from recognizing the self-evident truth that real goods ought to be desired.

Even though it cannot be a terminal goal reached and enjoyed, the ideal of a good life functions as all other ends do by prescribing certain means that we must employ and proscribing other things that we must eschew in order to pursue the ultimate good of our lives effectively. Happiness cannot be achieved by any means whatsoever, but only by choices and actions that add real goods to our life and that avoid apparent goods that interfere with the attainment of real goods.

To think, as is so widely believed today, that happiness consists in achieving whatever apparent goods an individual happens to desire according to his wants, without regard to the difference between right and wrong desires, leads to opposite conclusions all along the line. The ultimate good ceases to be the same ideal for all human beings. It ceases to be the common good of mankind. It functions as a terminal goal that can be completely achieved at some moment of one's life, not just approximated in some measure or degree in the course of a whole lifetime.

In addition, it becomes difficult if not impossible to understand how a good society, through the justice of its institutions and arrangements, can serve to promote the pursuit of happiness by all its members, differing as they do in their individual wants and more often than not brought into conflict with one another in their effort to satisfy them. It becomes meaningless to say that the state and its government should serve the common good of its people, for the happiness they strive for is no longer a common good.

No government or society can undertake to fulfill the obligation expressed in the maxim "To each according to his individual wants." The pursuit of happiness can be aided and abetted by just laws and institutions only to the extent that the state can do whatever may be necessary to provide all its members with the conditions requisite for fulfilling their common human needs. Over and above this, it should also permit them to satisfy their individual wants if doing so does not impede or frustrate others in their pursuit of happiness.

A single marvelously succinct statement by St. Augustine puts all of this in a nutshell. "Happy is the man," Augustine said, "who, in the course of a complete life, has everything he desires, provided he desire nothing amiss."

That kernel of wisdom calls for some expansion to make fully explicit the insight it contains. To desire nothing amiss is to desire only what one ought to desire and to refrain from desiring what one ought not to desire. The pursuit of happiness, properly conceived, puts us under the categorical obligation to seek everything that is really good for us and nothing that interferes with the attainment of all the real goods that fulfill our human needs.

To discharge this obligation, we must form the habit of choice that consists in desiring aright and desiring nothing amiss. We must aim at happiness, which is the ultimate good of our lives, and choose aright the means of achieving it.

That right aim conjoined with that right habit of choice constitute what the ancients called moral virtue. This is only one of the two indispensable factors in the pursuit of happiness. The other is the good fortune of being blessed by external circumstances that facilitate rather than frustrate its pursuit, especially with regard to the goods of chance partly or wholly beyond our control.

Aristotle's definition of happiness includes both of these factors and indicates that they are complementary: "Happiness consists in a complete life (i) lived in accordance with virtue *and* (ii) attended by a moderate supply of external goods" (or whatever goods depend in whole or in part on good fortune).

The individual may be a good person in the sense of being virtuous. But a good person does not always succeed in the pursuit of happiness—in making a good life for himself or herself. Virtue by itself does not suffice for the attainment of the ultimate good. If it did, mankind would have little or no reason to carry on its age-old struggle for a good society, with liberty, equality, and justice for all.

CHAPTER 14

From Truth and Goodness to Beauty

IN DEALING WITH TRUTH, and in response to an extreme skepticism that treated truth as if it were totally subjective and relative to the individual's opinions, we distinguished an objective aspect in which truth is universal and immutable from a subjective aspect in which individual claims to have a hold on the truth vary from individual to individual and from time to time.

In addition, we separated the sphere of truth from the sphere of taste. In the former, agreement is to be sought and engaging in argument can serve this purpose. In the latter, differences of opinion should be tolerated and there is no point in arguing to overcome them.

In dealing with goodness, and once again in response to an extreme skepticism that treated goods as if they were totally

subjective and relative to the individual's desires, we found a
parallel to the objective and subjective aspects of truth.

Real goods, we found, are relative not to individual desires,
but to desires inherent in human nature and so are the same for
all human beings. To the extent that human nature is everywhere and at all times the same (that is, as long as the species
persists in its specific characteristics), real goods have the universality and immutability that gives them objectivity. The
sameness of human nature at all times and places is usually
concealed from us by the overlays of nurture and culture, but
these can be stripped away and the common underlying nature
laid bare.

Another way of making the same point is to say that, while
many value judgments belong in the sphere of taste, some belong to the sphere of truth. Prescriptive judgments about the
real goods that ought to be desired because they fulfill our natural needs have a truth that differs from the truth of descriptive
judgments about the way things are in reality. About these
value judgments, we should seek agreement, and when we disagree, we should try to overcome our differences by resorting
to argument—by appeal to evidence and by reasoning. The
evidence will be drawn from and the reasoning will be about
our knowledge of human nature and our understanding of it.

The subjective aspect of goodness falls on the other side of
the line that divides real from apparent goods. Apparent goods
are relative to individual desires and are, therefore, subjective.
When, wanting something, the individual calls it good, that is
an expression of taste on his part, not a judgment that he should
expect others to agree with or about which he should engage in
argument with others.

Two things emerge from this review of ground we have been
over. One is the sovereignty of truth in relation to goodness
and, as we shall soon see, also in relation to beauty. The discovery that oughts can be true enables us to draw the line between
the objective and subjective aspects of goodness. It places our

judgments about real goods in the sphere of truth, and our opinions about apparent goods in the sphere of taste.

The other thing to emerge is the reason there is an objective as well as a subjective aspect of both truth and goodness. It is not the same reason in both cases.

The objectivity of truth derives from the existence of a reality that is independent of our minds and of our thinking about it. Since we attain truth by bringing our thought into agreement with the reality we try to know, that reality provides the standard whereby our thought is measured and is found true or false. The subjectivity of truth derives from the fallibility and deficiencies or inadequacies of human thought.

Goodness does not have objectivity in the same way, for our judgments concerning the good do not have truth by agreement with the reality we seek to know. With regard to real goods, what takes the place of objectivity is the intersubjectivity of human needs, which is to say their sameness for all human beings because they are inherent in human nature. Here it is human nature (which, of course, is a reality to be known) that provides the standard whereby our value judgments—our oughts—can be found true or false.

When we come to beauty, the same interest persists—the concern with what is objective and what is subjective in our attribution of beauty to things. That is the focal concern with regard to all three of these great ideas, but we can anticipate encountering greater difficulty in our effort to treat beauty in a manner that parallels our treatment of truth and goodness.

The reason for this should be immediately apparent. In the case of truth, one and the same reality measures our success in trying to arrive at true judgments about what does or does not exist or about the characteristics of that which does exist. In the case of goodness, one and the same human nature measures our success in trying to arrive at true judgments about the goods everyone needs and therefore the goods that everyone ought to desire. But, in the case of beauty, where shall we look for the common measure of our success in trying to arrive at true judgments about what is or is not beautiful?

There is still another reason for puzzlement. "Beauty is truth, truth beauty," it has been said; "that is all ye know on earth and all ye need to know." We have also been told, "Take care of truth and goodness, and beauty will take care of itself."

These remarks suggest that beauty is so related to truth and goodness that these other ideas should be able to guide us in our consideration of beauty. Despite the poet's vision of the matter, beauty is not identical with truth, at least not in the sense in which we have considered truth so far—as a property of propositions or statements.

Beauty would appear to be more intimately related to goodness. The reason for thinking so lies in the fact that beauty, like goodness, is a quality we attribute to things because of a relation they have to us. Both the good and the beautiful please us. Beauty may be a special type of goodness or it may be radically distinct from goodness.

We must find out which is the case. Only after we have discovered how the reason for our attribution of beauty to things differs from the reason for our attribution of goodness to them, can we proceed to the more difficult question about the objectivity and subjectivity of beauty.

CHAPTER 15

Enjoyable Beauty

MUCH HAS BEEN SAID on the subject of beauty that will not bear close scrutiny. What is said is often moving, even uplifting. It frequently gives one the sense of being on the verge of getting at the heart of the matter, but like epigrammatic discourse at its best, it leaves one unsure that the promise of penetrating insights can be fulfilled by patient thought expressed in plain speech.

The test of the intelligibility of any statement that overwhelms us with its air of profundity is its translatability into language that lacks the elevation and verve of the original statement but can pass muster as a simple and clear statement in ordinary, everyday speech. Most of what has been written about beauty will not survive this test. In the presence of many of the most eloquent statements about beauty, we are left speechless—

speechless in the sense that we cannot find other words for expressing what we think or hope we understand.

This is not to say that, in the discussion of the great ideas, there has been more disagreement about beauty than about truth and goodness. With regard to beauty as with regard to truth and goodness, the same fundamental issues are argued, issues concerning their objectivity and subjectivity. The difference lies in the fact that with regard to truth and goodness, the issues can be addressed with a clarity that is lacking in the case of beauty.

There is less that can be said about beauty with clarity and precision than can be said about truth and goodness. In the pages that follow, I am going to limit myself to observations that can be expressed in the language of common speech and to distinctions that I think are immediately intelligible to common sense.

I will carry the analysis no further than it can go within these limits. This may leave many questions unanswered for the reader, but he or she will at least understand the questions that have not been answered.

In the tradition of Western thought, two writers—and only two—provide the guidance we need to proceed along the lines just indicated. One is a thirteenth-century theologian, Thomas Aquinas; the other, an eighteenth-century German philosopher, Immanuel Kant. While these two do not agree with each other on all points, certain observations made by Kant help us to understand certain words used by Aquinas that are critical terms in his definition of the beautiful.

"The beautiful," Aquinas writes, "is that which pleases us upon being seen." In this definition of the beautiful, the two critical terms are "pleases" and "seen."

Many things please us and please us in different ways, but everything that pleases us is not beautiful. If we use the word "pleases" as a synonym for "satisfies," then any good that we desire pleases or satisfies us when, coming into possession of that good, our desire for it is calmed, put to rest, or made quiescent.

Pleasure itself, bodily or sensual pleasure, is among the goods that human beings desire. We have a natural craving for sensory experiences that have the quality of being pleasant rather than unpleasant. It is also the case that some human beings, generally regarded as abnormal, have a predilection for pain—for physical pain or for sensory experiences that are unpleasant in quality rather than pleasant. When these desires, normal or abnormal, are gratified, we are pleased or satisfied.

When sensual pleasure or pain is an object of desire, it does not differ from food or drink, wealth or health, knowledge or friendship, as something needed or wanted. Anything needed or wanted is something that pleases or satisfies us when we get it. How, among all the things that please or satisfy us, shall we identify the special character of the beautiful as an object that pleases us?

The answer to this question can be found in Aquinas's definition. The object we call beautiful is one that pleases us in a very special way—"upon being seen." Food and drink, health and wealth, and most of the other goods we need or want please us upon being possessed. It is having them, to use or consume, that pleases us. They please us when they satisfy our desire to *have* them, not just to *see* them.

Here Kant throws light on the special character of the pleasure afforded by objects we call beautiful by telling us that the pleasure must be a totally disinterested one. What Kant means by "disinterested" is that the object falls outside the sphere of our practical concerns. It is an object we may or may not desire to acquire, to possess, to use, consume, or in some other way incorporate into our lives or ourselves. We may be quite content simply to contemplate or behold it. Doing just that, and nothing more, gives us the special delight or joy that we derive from objects that please us upon being seen. And if, in addition, we do desire to possess it, we do not regard it as beautiful because of that fact.

A person can find a natural landscape or a painting in a gallery enjoyable in this special way without also having any practical interest in acquiring the real estate or the work of art that would make the enjoyable a permanent possession. The impulse of the buyer or collector may arise from the wish to have the object regarded as beautiful under one's control, but that wish may have a different motivation.

The same individual may be a connoisseur and a collector, but he or she can be a collector without being a connoisseur, relying on the judgment of others concerning the enjoyability of the thing in question.

It is also true that connoisseurs need not be collectors. Most of us are neither. We neither claim to have an expert or privileged position in judging which things to call beautiful, nor, when we find things that we enjoy with disinterested pleasure, do we also wish to possess them exclusively for ourselves.

The other troublesome point in Aquinas's definition of the beautiful lies in the word "seen." Do we derive disinterested pleasure only from visual objects—things that we apprehend by the use of our eyes? That can hardly be the case, for, if it were, it would exclude musical compositions and poetry of all sorts from the realm of the beautiful. It would also exclude what is sometimes referred to as the purely intelligible beauty of a mathematical demonstration or a scientific theory.

The trouble we confront here is not solely due to the use of the word "seen" by Aquinas in his definition of the beautiful. In our everyday speech and thought we tend to locate the beautiful in the realm of the visible. We tend to put "beautiful" into the company of other adjectives that apply exclusively or primarily to objects we apprehend by our sense of sight, such as "good-looking," "pretty," "handsome," "attractive in appearance." The oft repeated remark that beauty lies in the *eye* of the beholder confirms this inveterate tendency on our part.

This is not to say that any of us would identify the beautiful with objects that are merely good-looking, pretty, handsome, or visually attractive. We are given to saying that someone is good-looking, pretty, or handsome, but not beautiful. Nevertheless, our habits of speech reveal that we are also given to thinking that the beautiful is the superlative degree of a quality that is to be found in visual objects that are good-looking, pretty, or handsome. All give us *disinterested* pleasure upon being *seen*, but we reserve the word "beautiful" for that which pleases us to the highest degree and most exceptionally.

This tendency is further confirmed by the way that most of us use the word "art" or the phrase "fine arts." What in English we call the fine arts are called *beaux arts* in French or *schöne kunst* in German (i.e., "arts of the beautiful"), and we think of the *objets d'art* (the objects produced by these arts) as things hung on the walls of museums or placed on pedestals there.

The familiar phrase "literature, music, and the fine arts" would, accordingly, exclude poetry and music from the arts of the beautiful. This tendency carries over into the sphere of nature, where we find the beautiful mainly, if not exclusively, in scenes (landscapes, seascapes) or in trees, flowers, or animals that please us upon being seen.

How shall we correct this tendency, as we must if we are to accord to sonnets and sonatas the possibility of their being regarded as beautiful, even if the disinterested pleasure they afford us has nothing to do with their being seen? The answer is that the word "see" does not always mean "apprehend visually." All of us have said, "I see what you mean," in order to convey to another person that we understand what he or she has told us. Here the seeing is with the mind, not with the eyes alone, though the eyes may be involved if the statement to be understood is a written one; yet they need not be involved if the statement is a spoken one.

Another way of transcending the narrowly optical connotation of the word "seen" is to remember that we often refer to the vision of a great reformer or religious leader, when the vision in question is the contemplation of an ideal to be achieved. It is certainly not a sensory experience involving our eyes.

The Latin word "visum" which Aquinas used in his definition of the beautiful (*id quod visum placet*, that which pleases upon being seen) has the broader connotation of vision in the sense of contemplating an object that cannot be seen with the eyes, as is the case with an inspiring ideal or what, in Christian theology, is called the beatific vision—the contemplation of God that is vouchsafed souls that are saved.

To make our understanding of the matter secure, let us eliminate that troublesome word "seen," and substitute for it words that do not have a restrictive sensory connotation. We can then rephrase the definition in one of the following ways.

The beautiful is that which pleases us upon being contemplated. It is that which pleases us when we apprehend it with our minds alone, or, if not by our minds alone, then by our minds in conjunction with our senses, but not by the sense of sight alone. We might even say that the beautiful is something that it pleases us to behold, but only if we remember that we can behold something in other ways than by sight.

The pleasure in any case must be, as Kant observed, a disinterested pleasure. We are simply pleased by contemplating, apprehending, or beholding the object. Nothing more is required for us to experience the delight or enjoyment that must be present when we call the object beautiful.

Kant not only helps us to understand the term "pleases" in Aquinas's definition by introducing the notion of a purely disinterested pleasure. He also helps us to understand the kind of knowing that is involved in the vision of the beautiful—the special kind of knowing that is contemplating or beholding, the special mode of apprehending that is appropriate to an object that gives us disinterested pleasure when we apprehend it.

The apprehension, Kant declares, is devoid of concepts. The kind of knowledge that is expressed in scientific and philosophical judgments, in the conclusions of historical research, and in the generalizations that most of us are given to making in the course of our daily lives, is not devoid of concepts. Judgments that involve concepts are judgments that apply to kinds or classes of objects; even when they are judgments about an individual object, concepts are involved to the extent that the individual is regarded as a particular instance of this or that kind.

An apprehension totally devoid of conceptual content must, therefore, have for its object a unique individual, an individual that is not regarded as a particular instance of any class or kind, but is apprehended for and in itself alone.

When an object that we apprehend (contemplate or behold) gives us the purely disinterested pleasure that is derived simply from knowing it, the knowing is not scientific, philosophical, historical, or even ordinary commonsense knowing. It is the very special kind of knowing that eschews all conceptual ingredients, and is, therefore, a knowledge of the individual as such —just this one thing, unclassified, not one of a kind.

All the objects to which we stand in some relation can be placed in two main categories. On the one hand, they are objects of desire, objects we need, want, or love, objects of practical interest, objects with respect to which we take one or another sort of action. On the other hand, they are objects of knowledge, objects of perception, memory, and thought, objects of conceptual knowledge or objects of nonconceptual apprehension or contemplation. Goodness, as we have seen, is the value appropriate to the sphere of desire; truth, the value appropriate to the sphere of knowledge. Beauty, it would seem, belongs to both spheres, and to each in a very special way.

The term "pleases" in the definition of the beautiful places it in the sphere of desire, but since the pleasure is of the very special sort that Kant calls "disinterested," the desire is also of a very special sort—a desire to know. The knowing, as we have seen, is also of a very special sort—a nonconceptual contemplation or apprehension of the individual object as such. Nevertheless, since it is a mode of knowing, however special in character, beauty is a value that is appropriate to the same sphere in which we find truth, as well as a value that is appropriate to the same sphere in which we find goodness.

More remains to be said about beauty in relation to truth and goodness. Our understanding of beauty so far raises one question that we must hold before us as we proceed. So far, it would appear to be the case that beauty is entirely subjective. Defined as the property of any object that gives us the disinterested pleasure we can derive from simply contemplating or apprehending that individual object as such, beauty would appear to be entirely relative to the taste of the person pleased. As persons differ in their tastes, so they differ with respect to what affords them pleasure when they apprehend it.

We have found it possible to separate the sphere of truth from the sphere of taste. We have found it possible to distinguish real from apparent goods. This has enabled us to differentiate the objective from the subjective aspects of truth and goodness. Can we do the same in the case of beauty? Hardly, if the beautiful is strictly identical with the enjoyable—with that which gives us joy or delight when we apprehend it.

Many of us who enjoy something in this way and, therefore, call it beautiful may wish to think that everyone else ought to enjoy it, too. But we have no right to impose our taste on others unless we can find grounds for prescribing oughts in the sphere of the enjoyable. Even if such grounds cannot be found, we may still find that beauty is not entirely in the eye—or the mind —of the beholder.

CHAPTER 16

Admirable Beauty

WHEN, WANTING SOMETHING, I call it good, the statement that
the object wanted appears good to me is a statement primarily
about me and about the object only in relation to me. Unless
you suspect that I am trying to deceive you about my desire in
this instance, you will accept my statement as true.

You may, however, challenge it by telling me that what appears good to me is not really good, but the very opposite. You
would then be making a statement about the object, not about
me, a statement the truth of which you and I might reasonably
argue about.

If I call something beautiful because I derive pleasure simply
from beholding or contemplating it, that statement is also a
statement primarily about me and about the object only in relation to me. Eliminating any suspicion of deception on my
part, you will accept my statement as true.

Here, however, you cannot challenge it by telling me that the object in which I find beauty is not really enjoyable by me, but the very opposite. You may say that it gives you no pleasure to contemplate it, but this difference of opinion between us is a difference in taste that is not worth arguing about.

If the beautiful is identified with the enjoyable—with that which affords us the kind of enjoyment that is the purely disinterested pleasure derived from contemplating the object—there is no escaping the conclusion we have reached that beauty lies entirely in the eye of the beholder and is merely a matter of taste. But there is another sense in which, when we call an object beautiful, we are speaking about the object itself, and not about ourselves or about the object in relation to us.

We call the object beautiful because it has certain properties that make it admirable. It has those properties whether or not its having them results in its being enjoyable by you or me. If the admirable were universally enjoyable, then beautiful objects would always be subjectively experienced as beautiful also; that is, everyone would derive pleasure or enjoyment from contemplating them. But that is not the case, as everyone knows.

What remains to be seen, however, is whether there is any relation between the admirability of the object and its enjoyability by individuals differing in their temperaments, sensibilities, nurture, and culture. It should be noted, in any case, that admiration is just as much an expression of taste as enjoyment is; but with one difference. Enjoyment is immediate. Admiration may be mediated by thought and dependent upon knowledge.

The properties that make an object admirable have been variously named by writers about beauty.

Aristotle wrote, "To be beautiful, a living creature, and every whole made up of parts, must not only present a certain order in its arrangement of parts, but also be of a certain definite magnitude. Beauty is a matter of size and order. . . ."

Aquinas said that the beautiful object is one that has unity, proportion, and clarity. It is a complex whole having parts. When the parts are so organized and proportioned to one another that the complex structure of its wholeness is perspicuous or manifest (i.e., not obscured by any discordant or inharmonious element), the object thus constituted is beautiful. It is admirable for its intrinsic excellence or perfection.

Children used to be taught that in order to write a good composition, one that has intrinsic excellence or perfection, they should try to produce one that has unity, clarity, and coherence. In carpentry shops, they were, and still may be, taught that to make a good chair or table, they have to put the parts together in a way that produces a well-organized whole in which the parts are properly proportioned to one another. A poorly made chair may not be useful in serving the purpose for which chairs are made; but, quite apart from the question of its usefulness, a poorly made chair is not admirable. It lacks the perfection or intrinsic excellence of a well-made chair.

What has just been said about pieces of writing and products of carpentry applies to all works of human art—all man-made objects. Some may be made for use, as chairs and tables are. Some may be made for the enjoyment of contemplators, as poems, statues, paintings, and symphonies are. Some may be made for both use and enjoyment, as buildings are.

Sometimes an object made for use may become one that is contemplated with enjoyment, as a fine piece of furniture roped off in a museum. Sometimes an object made for enjoyment by contemplators may become one that is used for some practical purpose, as a painting hung to cover a stain on the wall.

But, regardless of the purpose for which it is made, how it is made, or how it is employed, anything that a human being makes is either well made or poorly made. It either has or lacks the intrinsic excellence or perfection that is appropriate to that kind of thing. It either is admirable or not.

If we turn from works of art to the things of nature, we speak of those that have intrinsic excellence or perfection as being well formed, not well made. Striking deformities are to be

found among all living things. Horticulturists root out de-
formed growths or try to correct them. Animal breeders eliminate from the breeding process the less well formed in order to
produce more perfect specimens of the kind in question.

At flower shows and dog or cat shows, judges award blue
ribbons or gold medals to the best of kind or breed—the rose
or orchid, the dog or cat that is more admirable for its intrinsic
excellence or perfection as that kind of living organism. The
winning specimen is declared to possess all the qualities that
an individual instance of that kind should have, and to be devoid of any blemishes or flaws.

The beautiful as the admirable is the same in works of art
and the things of nature. In both spheres, the object admired
as beautiful possesses an intrinsic excellence or perfection that
is appropriate to that kind of thing, whether a product of nature
or of art. The only difference is that in the sphere of art, we
speak of the admirable as the well-made; in the sphere of nature, we speak of it as the well-formed.

It may be pointed out that the flowers, dogs, or cats exhibited
at shows or fairs are not purely products of nature, since human
effort has intervened to achieve the perfection of breeding or
development that may win a prize. That, however, does not
affect the point under consideration. The admirable perfection
of the well-formed organism is often found in nature untouched
by human hands.

Acquiescing in everything that has been said so far, the
reader may interpose questions that certainly deserve to be
asked. Who says what is admirable or not? The judgment that
an object is admirable for its intrinsic excellence or perfection
may be a judgment about the object itself, about the properties
it possesses, but does that make the judgment objective rather
than subjective? Is it a judgment that has objective truth—one
that belongs in the sphere of truth rather than in the sphere of
taste and so one that is worth arguing about to get at the truth
of the matter?

To the first question—Who says what is admirable?—the answer has already been indicated. It is the English teacher, not the student, who judges whether the composition turned in has the unity, clarity, and coherence required for the production of a well-made piece of writing. It is the carpentry instructor, not the student, who judges whether or not the table or chair turned out in shop is admirable for the intrinsic excellence of a well-made chair or table. So, too, in all exhibits of living organisms in which entries compete for prizes, the awards are made by experts selected for their competence as judges to determine the most admirable or beautiful of the specimens exhibited.

The judgment about the beauty of an object in terms of its admirability for intrinsic excellence or perfection is the judgment of an expert, with special knowledge and skill in judging specimens of a certain kind. One would not ask the English teacher to judge the products of the carpentry shop, or the carpentry instructor to judge English compositions. One would not ask the judges selected for a dog or cat show to judge the roses or orchids exhibited at a flower show.

This is not to say that the experts cannot disagree. They often do, and the awards are, therefore, made by averaging the points given the objects by a panel of judges. The spectators may also disagree with the final results, thinking that the specimen awarded second place is more admirable than the one given the blue ribbon or gold medal as the most beautiful object of its kind. But there is a difference between the disagreement of the experts with one another and the disagreement between the laymen and the experts.

The skilled judges can argue reasonably with one another about the points scored by the specimens under consideration; it is quite possible for such argument to result in a change of opinion and an altered final result. But the layman cannot argue with the judges in a way that might persuade them to change their minds. If he could, he would be an expert himself, not a layman.

In the sphere of the fine arts—the arts called, in French and German, the arts of the beautiful—there are also expert judges and mere laymen who lack the knowledge and skill possessed by the expert in a particular field of art. The persons who are acknowledged literary or musical critics, or connoisseurs of painting and sculpture, may differ more frequently or more radically in their opinions about the admirable beauty of a particular work than do the judges at flower, dog, or cat shows. But it still remains the case that they are in a position to argue reasonably with one another, with the hope that one can persuade another to change his opinion, whereas mere laymen cannot argue with them, either reasonably or fruitfully.

Is, then, the judgment of beauty that is based on the admirability of an object for its intrinsic excellence or perfection a matter of truth or a matter of taste? The answer depends on how we answer another question. Does the distinction that is generally acknowledged between the mere laymen and the skilled, knowledgeable expert in a particular field carry with it acknowledgment of a difference between inferior and superior taste?

Must it not be the case that to have superior taste is to have the ability to perceive correctly the superiority of one object over another for its intrinsic excellence or perfection? What would superior taste mean if the person having it could not make a reasonable and well-grounded judgment about which of two objects was the more admirable?

In short, must we not conclude that, though judgments about the admirable beauty of objects are expressions of taste on the part of those who make such judgments, expert judges have superior taste that enables them to rank objects correctly in a way that accords with the degree to which they possess intrinsic excellence or perfection?

That conclusion has two corollaries. The first is that, while judgments of the admirable beauty of objects are expressions of taste, they are also judgments that can have a certain measure of objective truth—judgments about which reasonable and profitable argument can occur among experts. *De gustibus non disputandum est* does not apply to the experts in a particular field.

The second corollary is that the degrees of admirable beauty attributed to objects is objective, not subjective; that is, it pertains to the condition of the object, not to the state of mind or feeling of the subject making the judgment. If one object were not in its intrinsic properties superior to another, the person who judged it as the more admirable could not be said to have superior taste as compared with the person who made the opposite judgment. Only if there are gradations of excellence or perfection in the objects themselves, making one more admirable than another, can there be gradations in the scale of taste, making expert judges superior to laymen and, even among experts, making one judge superior to another.

Those who hold the view that beauty is objective rather than subjective go further and assert a third corollary; namely, that the more admirable or beautiful an object is in itself, the more enjoyable it must be *universally*—to all human beings at all times and places and under all circumstances of nurture and culture. What is objectively beautiful because of its admirable intrinsic excellence or perfection must also be subjectively beautiful, enjoyable or pleasing to all who behold or contemplate it.

The view just set forth cannot be defended. The objective and subjective aspects of beauty are not correlated. That which, in the judgment of experts in a particular field, may be admirable beauty in an object is not always and uniformly enjoyable. It may please one individual who contemplates it, and not another. In fact, to acknowledge that some individuals are persons of poor or uncultivated taste is to recognize that they are likely to enjoy less rather than more admirable objects.

If a person's taste can be cultivated and improved with regard to a certain kind of object, the individual is more likely to enjoy objects that, in the judgment of experts, are more admirable. But this does not alter the basic fact that enjoyable beauty is one thing and admirable beauty another.

The individual who derives disinterested pleasure from the contemplation of objects that lack intrinsic excellence or perfection, or have an inferior degree of it, is thoroughly justified in regarding such objects as beautiful because they provide the enjoyment appropriate to calling them beautiful. They have for that individual the beauty of the enjoyable even if they lack the beauty of the admirable in the judgment of experts, or persons of superior taste.

Because there are these two distinct senses in which objects can be called beautiful (as admirable and as enjoyable), beauty has both an objective and a subjective dimension. The trouble is that the two dimensions do not run parallel to one another.

Much of the confusion that is prevalent in discussions of beauty comes from not recognizing this fact. The person who calls an object beautiful because he enjoys it is often interpreted as meaning that it is also admirable because of its intrinsic excellence or perfection. That individual often misinterprets his own expression of subjective taste as possessing an objective significance that it does not have.

Many of us as laymen in a given field would like to think that an object that pleases us should be equally enjoyable to others. We often go so far as to say that they ought to enjoy what we enjoy. Expert judges in a given field of objects are even more disposed to say that everyone ought to enjoy the objects they judge more admirable for the beauty of their intrinsic excellence or perfection, or at least to recommend that everyone's taste ought to be cultivated and improved to the point where they would find the more admirable also more enjoyable.

Prescriptive oughts do not apply to enjoyment. No one can tell another person what he ought or ought not to enjoy, as one can tell another what he ought or ought not to desire (because it is really good or really bad); or as one person can tell another what he ought or ought not to affirm as true (because evidence and reasoning support the proposition in question rather than its opposite, either beyond the shadow of a doubt, or beyond a reasonable doubt, or by a preponderance of evidence and reasons in its favor).

The only ought that would seem to be admissible in the sphere of the enjoyable is one that is an educational prescription. We think that education should result in the formation of a mind that thinks as it ought, judging correctly about the truth and falsity of propositions. We think that education should result in the formation of a virtuous moral character, one that desires aright or chooses as it ought with regard to good and evil. To carry this one step further, from the spheres of truth and goodness to the sphere of beauty, we need only say that education should result in the formation of good taste so that the individual comes to enjoy that which is admirable, and to derive more enjoyment from objects that have greater intrinsic excellence or perfection. Beyond this one cannot go. One cannot prescribe what everyone ought to find enjoyable because of its admirable intrinsic properties.

Not only must we acquiesce in the relativity of enjoyable beauty to the taste of the individual at whatever level of cultivation it may be. We must also recognize that enjoyable beauty is relative to the cultural circumstances of the individual as well as to his innate temperament and his nurture. Peoples of diverse cultures differ radically with respect to the objects in which they find enjoyable beauty. A Westerner in Japan may be left cold in the presence of a Zen garden or a Kabuki performance that the Japanese contemplate for hours with rapt enjoyment. A European may not find enjoyable beauty in African sculpture, or an African in Western abstract painting.

The relativity of beauty to cultural differences extends from enjoyable to admirable beauty. Those who have the expertness to make them competent judges of Western painting may be mere laymen when it comes to admiring Chinese or Japanese screens. Even within the broad scope of Western culture, experts competent to judge classical sculptures or Byzantine mosaics may not have comparable competence when it comes to admiring impressionist or postimpressionist paintings.

The person who says, as many do, "I do not know whether that object is beautiful, but I know what I like, and I do like it," should understand himself to be acknowledging the disconnection between enjoyable and admirable beauty. He is, in effect, saying, "I do not know what expert judges would think about the intrinsic excellence or perfection of the object in question, but I do know that it pleases me to behold or contemplate. It may or may not be admirable in the judgment of experts, but I enjoy it nevertheless."

There is one further difference to be noted between the expert judgment of admirable beauty and the expression of taste for enjoyable beauty, whether by experts or by laymen. It requires us to recall Immanuel Kant's observation that the apprehension of an object from which we derive disinterested pleasure is nonconceptual. It is the apprehension or contemplation of that individual object as such, not as a particular instance of one or another kind of object.

Contrariwise, the expert judgment of the admirable beauty of an object based on its intrinsic excellence or perfection cannot be a judgment devoid of conceptual content because it is always a judgment about the individual object, *not as an individual*, but as a particular instance of a certain kind.

The knowledge that is involved in being an expert is knowledge about the kind, specimens of which are being judged. The skill of the expert is skill in discriminating the degrees of excellence possessed by less and more admirable specimens of the kind in question. That is why the person who is an expert judge of Greek temples will probably not be an expert judge of Gothic cathedrals, and why the person who is an expert judge of flowers is unlikely to be an expert judge of dogs.

The objectivity of truth lies in the fact that what is true for an individual who happens to be in error is not true at all. The objectivity of goodness lies in the fact that what is called good by an individual whose wants are contrary to his needs is not really good for him or for anyone else. What is true for the person whose judgment is sound ought to be regarded as true by everyone else. What is good for the person whose desires are right ought to be regarded as good by everyone else.

When we come to beauty, the parallelism fails. What is enjoyable beauty for the individual whose taste is poor and who derives pleasure from inferior objects is really enjoyable beauty for him regardless of what anyone else thinks, including the experts. What is admirable beauty in the judgment of the experts may not be enjoyable beauty for many laymen; nor can we say that they ought to admire as well as enjoy it because of its intrinsic excellence. All we can say, perhaps, is that they ought to learn to enjoy what is admirable.

At the bottom line, it remains the case that the enjoyable belongs to the sphere of the subjective—a matter of individual taste about which there is no point in arguing. The best wine experts in the world may all agree that a certain red Bordeaux of a certain vintage is a supreme specimen of claret. It does not follow that an individual who prefers white wine to red, or Burgundies to clarets, or has a taste for whiskey rather than for wine, must necessarily enjoy drinking the wine accorded the gold medal by the experts.

What is true of wines is true of everything else that, on the one hand, can be judged for its admirable intrinsic excellence and, on the other hand, may or may not give pleasure or enjoyment to the taste of individuals.

One concluding observation. Readers who feel dissatisfied or disappointed by what I have been able to say about admirable beauty—the intrinsic excellence of objects judged admirable by experts—have reason on their side. They are justified in expecting something more: a clear and precise statement of the features shared in common by all instances of admirable beauty, whether in nature or in works of art, and in any and every sphere of art.

I sympathize with such dissatisfaction or disappointment. I have suffered it myself. Expert judges in a given field of art may be able to state the underlying principles or criteria of intrinsic excellence in that sphere of workmanship. They seldom can do so unanimously. But even if they were all to agree about the objective criteria of admirable beauty in the field in which they were experts, even if they all subscribed to principles by conformity to which a judgment concerning the admirable beauty of a certain object could claim to be true, that would still be insufficient.

More can be reasonably expected of the philosopher who undertakes to deal with the idea of beauty. In dealing with the ideas of truth and goodness, the philosopher discharges his intellectual responsibility. He is able to tell us what truth and goodness consist in, not in some particular domain, but universally. That intellectual responsibility the philosopher does not seem able to discharge in dealing with the idea of beauty.

I would have wished to write this chapter in a philosophical manner not disappointing to its readers, not failing to provide the clear and precise statement about what beauty objectively consists in, which they have good reason to expect. I have failed for two reasons. One is that I am not able to find that clear and precise statement in the literature of the subject. The other is that I lack the insight or wisdom needed to supply it myself.

Disappointed readers must, therefore, convert their dissatisfaction by transforming it into a challenge—to do for themselves what has yet to be done by anyone. To do what? To say what is common to—what universal qualities are present in—the admirable beauty of a prize-winning rose, Beethoven's Kreutzer Sonata, a triple play in the ninth inning of a baseball game, Michelangelo's *Pieta*, a Zen garden, Milton's sonnet on his blindness, a display of fireworks, and so on.

CHAPTER 17

The Goodness of Beauty and the Beauty of Truth

IN THE MEDIEVAL CATALOGUE of the transcendental values, truth and goodness are among the six all-encompassing ideas accorded this status, but beauty is not. The reason given is that, viewed in one way, beauty is a special kind of goodness; and viewed in another, that kind of goodness is also a special kind of truth.

The special kind of goodness that is enjoyable beauty is marked by the character of the pleasure it affords—a purely disinterested pleasure. The ordinary things we regard as good please or satisfy us when we acquire or possess them, use or consume them. They are goods to have. We are practically interested in having them. The pleasure we get from having them is hardly disinterested.

In contrast, the enjoyable beauty of an object is a good we do not wish to acquire or possess; we are pleased simply to know it—to apprehend or contemplate it. Ordinary goodness and the special kind of goodness that is enjoyable beauty thus differ in the way in which the object is related to us.

When we consider the object in itself, quite apart from its relation to us, we are concerned with its admirable, not its enjoyable, beauty. As with enjoyable beauty, so with admirable beauty, beauty is a special kind of goodness.

All sorts of objects are ranked or graded according to the degree of their intrinsic excellence or perfection. As we observed in an earlier chapter, experts judge the merit of coffees, teas, wines, liquors of all sorts. The grading that results in a scale of merit can be interpreted as signifying which is most admirable for its intrinsic excellence as that kind of thing, and which others, in descending degrees, stand lower in the scale of admirability.

The degrees of admirable excellence or goodness that are assigned such consumable products as coffees or wines, or such usable products as knives, swords, or other tools, belong in the category of *goods to have*—goods we are interested in acquiring, either to consume or use. Admirable beauty is a special kind of admirable excellence or goodness. It belongs in the category of *goods to know*, not to have, consume, or use. The distinctive character of admirable beauty as a special kind of goodness, like that of enjoyable beauty, lies in the special way that the goodness of the object stands in relation to us.

Quite apart from its relation to us, the admirable excellence of an object (whether it is an object to acquire, for use or consumption, or an object to apprehend simply for the enjoyment of contemplating it) is a special kind of goodness in still another way. In an earlier chapter, we referred to this special kind of goodness as the goodness that is commensurate with the being of the thing itself.

The degree of such goodness that different modes of existence have is the same as the degree of being or existence that they have. That which has a higher grade of being, accompanied by more power to act and react, has commensurately a higher grade of existential goodness. As we observed, a pearl may be more valuable than a mouse, more valuable either for use or in exchange, but a mouse has more existential goodness than a pearl because, being a living organism, it has more power to act and react than an inert pebble. It is better to be a mouse than a pearl. Existential goodness belongs in the category of the *good to be,* quite different from the *good to have,* the *good to do,* or the *good to know.*

The lower and higher grades of existential goodness that are exemplified by the comparison of a mouse and a human being represent a ranking that involves different kinds, species, or modes of being. Within a given kind, species, or mode of being, individual instances or specimens of that kind can also be graded for their intrinsic excellence or perfection.

That is precisely what is done by those who grade wines and coffees, knives, swords, and other tools for their degree of admirable excellence as things to be consumed or used. It is also precisely what is done by the expert judges who award blue ribbons or gold medals at flower or dog shows. They, too, are grading objects for their admirable excellence as objects, not to be used or consumed but rather as objects to behold with enjoyment.

In both cases, the degree of admirable excellence attributed to the object by the ranking accorded it is its degree of goodness as an instance or specimen of that kind of thing. The most admirable rose or orchid is the rose or orchid that conforms most perfectly to the idea of a rose or orchid. Perhaps we should say that it best exemplifies the ideal rose or orchid. It is everything that a rose or orchid ought to be. It has all the perfections that should belong to being a rose or an orchid.

Theology provides us with an understanding of this special kind of goodness. It cannot be obtained from any other way of thinking about things. The ranking of pearls, mice, and men as having degrees of existential goodness commensurate with

their grade of being leads, of course, to the acknowledgment of
the supreme existential goodness of God as commensurate with
God's existence as the Supreme Being. The theologian goes
further. Thinking of God as the creator of things, he looks upon
each kind of thing and, within every kind, each individual
instance or specimen of that kind as the product of creative
ideas in the mind of God.

At this point, the theologian introduces the notion of a special kind of truth—an existential truth that is identical with the
existential goodness of things. Our ordinary notion of truth
places truth in the mind of man when what it thinks conforms
to the way things are. But, the theologian tells us, there is also
a truth in things themselves, an existential truth that they possess when things conform to creative ideas in the mind of God.

Hence, when we say of the perfect rose or orchid that it is
everything that a rose or orchid should be, its admirable intrinsic excellence consists in its having a perfection that is at once
existential goodness and existential truth by conformity with
the ideal that is the idea of a rose or orchid in the mind of God.

Those who are inclined to dismiss theology for one reason or
another can grasp the same point by substituting for creative
ideas in the mind of God regulative ideals in the mind of man.
Turning our attention from the things of nature to works of art,
the substitution looks to the creative ideas in the mind of the
artist. One aspect of the intrinsic excellence of a work of art—
its existential goodness and truth—derives from the degree to
which it conforms to the creative idea in the mind of its maker.

There is one judgment that the artist and only the artist can
make. Only the artist can say whether the work produced is
true to the creative idea from which it issued. Only the artist
can judge how good it is in the sense of its being a faithful
execution of what he or she had in mind.

However, when the artist's work is judged by others for its
intrinsic excellence, the conformity of the object to the idea in
the artist's mind and the fidelity of his or her execution of that
idea are by no means enough. These are not the only consider-

ations, nor are they ever the main considerations. The objective critic of the artist's work, as compared with the artist himself or herself, is more concerned with the goodness of the creative idea as represented in the work produced by it.

The contemplation of enjoyable beauty consists, as we have seen, in a special kind of knowing—the nonconceptual apprehension of the individual object as such. So, too, the judgment by the artist himself of the admirable beauty of his work is a special kind of judgment—a judgment of the individual work with reference only to the creative idea that produced it. The judgment of the admirable beauty of the same work by the expert who is not the artist is a judgment that involves a conceptual framework—an understanding of the genre or kind to which the individual work belongs.

The admirable beauty of works of art that belong to different genres is incomparable. It is possible to say that a certain Greek temple or Gothic cathedral is more admirable than another, but one cannot say that the admirable beauty of a Gothic cathedral, for example, is greater or less than the admirable beauty of an Egyptian, Greek, or Romanesque temple. One cannot say that the admirable beauty of the Byzantine mosaics displayed in Ravenna or in Istanbul is greater or less than the admirable beauty of the impressionist paintings displayed in the Jeu de Paume in Paris. Even more incomparable is the admirable beauty of a building, a painting, a statue, a lyric, a drama, a novel, a song, a sonata, a symphony, a ballet, a motion picture, and so on.

Because of this, beauty differs radically from truth and goodness in one very important respect. Mankind can make progress in the pursuit of truth. Mankind can also make progress in the sphere of goodness, advancing from less to more perfect political, social, and economic institutions or arrangements. But there is no possibility of progress in the sphere of beauty.

The transition from Egyptian to Greek temples, from Greek to Romanesque temples, or from these to Gothic cathedrals is not an advance to greater perfection in the sphere of beauty as the transition from a society in which chattel slavery is a legally recognized institution to one in which chattel slavery has been legally abolished is an advance in the sphere of the goodness that is justice.

Finally, we come to the goodness of enjoyable beauty itself —its goodness as a good in human life that contributes to happiness.

Aristotle wisely observed that human beings cannot live without pleasure. Pleasure is a real good that satisfies one of man's basic inherent needs. Aristotle then goes on to point out that if human beings are deprived of the pleasures of the spirit, they are likely to indulge inordinately in the pleasures of the flesh.

Inordinate indulgence in the pleasures of the flesh involves wanting too much of one real good, and this can interfere with the acquirement of other real goods. Protection against such overindulgence comes from the spiritual—the disinterested— pleasure that we experience in the enjoyment of beauty.

The proposition that human beings cannot *live* without pleasure thus turns into the proposition that human beings cannot *live well* unless they moderate their pursuit of bodily pleasures by finding another and a different kind of pleasure in the enjoyment of beauty.

We must not allow ourselves to interpret this insight in a manner that tends to become elitist. The enjoyment of beauty is not confined to the lives of those who have the habit of visiting museums, attending concerts or ballets, going to the theater, or reading poetry. It occurs also in the lives of those who are baseball, basketball, or football fans, those who go to bullfights, those who watch tennis matches, and so on.

The sports spectator who, beholding an extraordinary play or action, cries out, "Wow, that's beautiful," is experiencing the same enjoyment or disinterested pleasure that is experienced by the auditor of an extraordinary performance of a Beethoven quartet or by the person who, if it were not impolite, would be inclined to cry out, "Wow, that's beautiful," when witnessing an extraordinary twist of the fan by an actor in a Kabuki drama or an extraordinary pas de deux by ballet dancers.

In addition, the sports enthusiast or fan is an expert judge of the intrinsic excellence or admirable beauty of a stunning triple play, or of a completed forward pass that scores a goal from a defensive position. So, too, the aficionado of the bullfight not only enjoys the beauty but is also an expert judge of the excellence of the picador's performance with his bandilleros, of the grace of the toreador in the handling of the cape, and of the matador's daring delivery of the final sword thrust that is fatal to the bull.

Their well-trained and highly cultivated taste in such matters makes them expert judges who applaud the beauty of the perfect or near-perfect play or performance. Compared with them, the rest of us are mere laymen or amateurs with little taste and even less expertness of judgment about what is admirable. Our deficiency here is comparable to our deficiency as laymen when compared with experts in the field of music, architecture, painting, or any other of the fine arts.

The goodness of enjoyable beauty lies in the disinterested pleasure it affords, regardless of the character of the object from which this pleasure is derived. The pleasure of contemplation is the pleasure of spectatorship, a pleasure that lifts us up from our practical involvement in the purposeful or interested activities that occupy the greater part of our daily lives. It might also be said to lift us out of ourselves, resulting in a kind of ecstasy.

Once again the theologian can provide us with an illuminating comment. Human life involves a number of distinct activities: sleeping and other biologically necessary activities, such as eating and drinking; working to obtain economic goods or the means of subsistence; playing for the fun of it; and leisuring for the improvement of one's mind.

Should we—can we—add resting, where resting is not to be identified with sleeping or relaxing or playing? Where can we find rest on earth, a rest that is remotely comparable to the heavenly rest of the souls who enjoy in heaven the beatific vision of God?

The contemplation of anything from which we derive the disinterested or spiritual pleasure of enjoyable beauty also introduces rest into our lives. The goodness of enjoyable beauty that makes it an indispensable ingredient in the happiness of a well-lived life consists in its providing us with the rest that all of us need.

To complete the picture, we must not forget that the restful experience of enjoyable beauty is not limited to the contemplation of sensible objects. We can experience it as well in the contemplation of purely intelligible objects—the contemplation of truths we understand. "Mathematics," wrote Bertrand Russell, "rightly viewed, possesses not only truth, but supreme beauty—a beauty cold and austere . . . without appeal to any part of our weaker nature, without the gorgeous trappings of painting or music . . ." Or, as the poet Edna St. Vincent Millay wrote in the opening line of her sonnet on Euclid, "Euclid alone has looked on beauty bare."

Considering the enjoyable beauty of truth, on the one hand, and, on the other hand, remembering that the admirable beauty of things having existential perfection is not only a special kind of goodness but also a special kind of truth, we may finally have reached some understanding of what Keats meant when he wrote, "Beauty is truth, truth beauty," even though it may not be true that that is "all ye know on earth and all ye need to know."

If the pursuit of happiness can be successfully conducted in the fullest measure only if we somehow manage to introduce into our lives enjoyable beauty and the rest that it affords us, does making a good life for ourselves require us to seek beauty wherever we can find it?

A negative answer to that question flows from a common experience that most of us will attest to. The enjoyment of beauty *happens* to us. We do not seek it out. We go to a baseball game, to a museum, or a concert, with the hope, perhaps, that the ecstatic moment will occur—the moment when, in one way or another, we exclaim our appreciation of the beautiful. But it does not always occur, and hoping that it will happen is not the same as seeking it out.

The most we can do in this direction is to expose ourselves to the opportunity for experiencing enjoyable beauty that is afforded by certain places, performances, events, or occasions. Whether that good befalls us or not is beyond our control. It is ultimately a good of chance rather than a good of choice.

PART THREE

Ideas We Act On: Liberty, Equality, and Justice

CHAPTER 18

The Sovereignty of Justice

IN TREATING THE IDEAS OF TRUTH, goodness, and beauty, I dealt with each in itself and for its own sake before considering its relation to the other two. Turning now to the remaining three of the six great ideas—liberty, equality, and justice—I will proceed somewhat differently. Though I will examine each of these ideas in and for itself, I will be primarily interested in those aspects of them in which they are closely interrelated. It is in those aspects that this triad of ideas are the ideas we act on in governing our social, political, and economic affairs.

In the case of the first three ideas, we observed the sovereignty of truth in the way it regulates our thinking about goodness and beauty. So here, in dealing with the second set of ideas, we must note the sovereignty of justice. It regulates our thinking about liberty and equality. Without its guidance, certain errors are unavoidable and certain problems insoluble.

It should also be pointed out that all three of these ideas fall in the domain of the idea of goodness. We rightly regard liberty and equality as highly desirable goods, real goods that we need to lead decent human lives in the pursuit of happiness. Just action with respect to others, as we saw in an earlier chapter, is the good of doing. To act rightly or justly is to do good.

It is necessary to explain the sovereignty of justice with regard to liberty and equality before we embark, in subsequent chapters, on elucidating these ideas as well as exploring in detail the idea of justice itself. Readers will appreciate, I trust, that their understanding of what is said briefly here will be increased by the light that subsequent chapters will throw on the subject.

In the popular mind, and even in the opinions of the learned, either liberty, or equality, or both together, is accorded the highest honor as the prime value or values to be sought, secured, and preserved. Much more inflamed rhetoric, as well as much more reasoned argument, has called for liberty above all else, or for equality above all else, or for both together, than there have been appeals for justice first and foremost.

The maxim of the French Revolution still echoes in our ears: *liberté, égalité, fraternité.* Justice is not even mentioned in the company of the other two. That might have been justified had the authors of that maxim written it on the basis of Aristotle's insight that if all human beings who are associated in a community were friends with one another, there would be no need for justice. It is doubtful that they had this in mind.

Against the weight of both popular and scholarly opinion, I will try to explain why justice is the supreme value, a greater good than either liberty or equality, and one that must be appealed to for the rectification of errors with regard to liberty and equality.

As I observed a moment ago, all three of these values are real, not apparent, goods—goods that human beings need for the conduct of their lives in the pursuit of happiness. However, all real goods are not of equal standing. Wealth and health, for example, are inferior to wisdom and friendship. Some real goods are truly good only when limited. Pleasure is a real good, but we can want more pleasure than we need or more than is good for us to seek or obtain. The same is true of wealth. These are limited real goods. In contrast, knowledge is an unlimited real good. We can never seek or obtain more than is good for us.

Only justice is an unlimited good, as we shall presently see. One can want too much liberty and too much equality—more than it is good for us to have in relation to our fellowmen, and more than we have any right to. Not so with justice. No society can be too just; no individual can act more justly than is good for him or for his fellowmen.

The failure to observe and understand the need for limitations upon liberty and equality leads to serious errors about them and to an irresolvable conflict between them.

On the one hand, there are the libertarians, who not only place the highest value on liberty but also seek to maximize it at the expense of equality. They not only want an unlimited amount of freedom, but they are also willing to try to achieve it even if achieving it results in an irremediable inequality of conditions, under which some portion of a society, usually a majority, suffer serious deprivations.

The only equality they are for is equality of opportunity, because this encourages and facilitates freedom of enterprise on the part of those who, favored by superior endowments or attainments, can make the best use of their freedom of opportunity to beat their fellowmen in the race of life—the devil take the hindmost! That a vast inequality of conditions will result does not deter them, for in their view trying to achieve an equality of conditions can only result in the loss of individual liberty, which is for them the higher of the two values.

On the other hand, there are the egalitarians, who not only

regard an equality of conditions as the supreme value, but also are set upon trying to achieve it even if that infringes in many ways on individual liberty, and especially upon freedom of enterprise, exercised with the help of equality of opportunity. In their view equality of opportunity, if that alone exists and if individual freedom in taking advantage of it is unrestrained, will necessarily result in an inequality of conditions. This they deplore. They seek to maximize an equality of conditions, even if to do so requires many infringements upon individual liberty, which is the lesser value in their view.

The conflict, not between liberty and equality, but between extremist exponents of these values, cannot be resolved without correcting the errors that lead to the extremisms respectively espoused by the libertarian and by the egalitarian. These errors can be corrected only by understanding that neither liberty nor equality is the prime value, that neither is an unlimited good, and that both can be maximized harmoniously only when the maximization is regulated by justice.

Should an individual have unlimited freedom of action or enterprise, or only as much liberty as he can use without injuring others, without depriving them of freedom, and without causing them to suffer the serious deprivations that are consequences of an inequality of conditions? In short, should an individual have more liberty than he can exercise justly?

Negative answers to these questions lead to the conclusion that everyone should have only as much liberty as justice allows, and no more than that.

Should a society try to achieve an equality of conditions attended by no inequalities in the degree to which individuals enjoy that equality of conditions? Should it seek to maximize such an equality of conditions, even if that results in serious deprivations of individual freedom? Should it ignore the fact that human beings are unequal as well as equal, in both their endowments and attainments, and that they make unequal contributions to the welfare of the community?

Negative answers to these questions lead to the conclusion

that a society should seek to achieve only as much of an equality of conditions as justice requires, and no more than that. More than that would be unjust, even as more freedom than justice allows would be an unjust exercise of liberty that is license.

The reader will have noted that justice stands in a different relation to liberty and to equality.

With respect to liberty, it imposes a limitation on the amount of individual freedom that it *allows*, if the exercise of freedom is to be just rather than unjust.

With respect to equality, it imposes a limitation on the kind and degree of the equality, as well as the kind and degree of the inequality, it *requires*, if a community is to deal justly with all its members.

When justice thus regulates the pursuit of liberty and equality, both can be maximized harmoniously within the limits set. The irresolvable conflict between the erroneous extremism of the libertarian and the erroneous extremism of the egalitarian vanishes. The sovereignty of justice has corrected the errors and resolved the conflict.

CHAPTER 19

The Freedom to Do as One Pleases

LIKE MOST OTHER GREAT IDEAS, liberty is not without its inner complexity. We have found that there are different kinds of truth, different modes of goodness, different senses of beauty. So, too, in the case of liberty or freedom. The two words are completely interchangeable.

There are three major forms of freedom. The first is a freedom that is inherent in human nature. We are born with it in our possession. It is distinctive of human beings, just as rational or conceptual thought and syntactical speech are distinctive of human beings. It is, therefore, appropriate to speak of it as a natural freedom, thus referring to the way in which we possess it.

The second major kind of liberty is the liberty that is associated with wisdom and moral virtue. It is possessed only by those who, in the course of their personal development, have acquired some measure of virtue and wisdom. Thus possessed, it is appropriately designated as an acquired freedom.

The third of the major forms of freedom is completely dependent on favorable external circumstances. An individual's possession of it may vary from time to time and from place to place, depending on whether external circumstances favorable or unfavorable to its exercise are present. Individuals may possess it or be deprived of it in varying degrees, which is certainly not the case with natural or acquired freedom. The appropriate way to designate this liberty is to speak of it as circumstantial freedom.

Described so far in terms of the way in which we possess them, what do these three forms of freedom or kinds of liberty consist in?

Our natural freedom consists in freedom of the will. It is freedom of choice—the liberty of being able to choose otherwise than as we did. Having such freedom, our actions are not instinctively determined or completely conditioned by the impact of external circumstances on our development, as is the case in the behavior of other animals. With this innate power of free choice, each human being is able to change his own character creatively by deciding for himself what he shall do or shall become. We are free to make ourselves whatever we choose to be.

Our acquired liberty, which is sometimes called "moral freedom," consists in our having a will that is habitually disposed by virtue to will as it ought. Virtue, as we have already seen, is the habitual disposition to desire aright, which means choosing what one needs—the real goods one ought to desire. The obstacles or impediments to right desire stem from appetites or passions that generate wants in conflict with needs, wants that tempt or solicit us to make the wrong rather than the right choices.

Human bondage, according to Spinoza, is our enslavement by such appetites or passions—our lower nature. Human freedom—moral liberty—lies in reason's control of the passions, made firm by moral virtue, the acquired habitual disposition to make right rather than wrong choices.

The freedom to will or choose as one ought could not be acquired by human beings if they did not antecedently possess, as an inherent property of human nature, a free will and the power of free choice. If we cannot choose otherwise, how can we be morally responsible for choosing aright rather than yielding to the seductions of pleasure or lust? And if we cannot be held morally responsible for the choices we make, what justification can there be for the praise or blame we accord an individual for his or her character or conduct?

Our circumstantial freedom consists in our being able to do as we please—our ability to carry out in overt action the decisions we have reached, to do as we wish for our individual good as we see it, rightly or wrongly.

Such freedom can be possessed and exercised by individuals of good or bad moral character. The individual's free choice of a line of conduct to pursue, or his decision about a course of action to take, may be morally virtuous or the opposite, but in either case, circumstances either permit him to behave or act as he wishes, or prevent him from doing so. Accordingly, the individual is either circumstantially free or unfree.

Our natural or inherent freedom of will confers upon us the power to choose otherwise—to make, on a particular occasion, a choice different from the one we made. Our circumstantial freedom of action, when we possess it in the fullest measure, confers upon us the ability to act otherwise. We are not only left free by favorable circumstances to enact the choice we made; we are also left free to enact a different, or opposite choice, had we made it.

An individual in prison or in chains is circumstantially free to remain in his cell or manacled, should that be his choice. But bars or chains prevent him from going elsewhere or doing otherwise if he wishes to. The restraints imposed by imprisonment impair his freedom of action, not his freedom of choice, and not his moral liberty—his freedom to will as he ought.

Two extraordinarily wise and virtuous human beings attest to this striking fact. The Roman Stoic philosopher Epictetus regarded himself as a free man, in the sense of having moral liberty, even though he was a slave in chains. So, too, the Christian philosopher Boethius eloquently celebrated his moral freedom in a discourse that he wrote in prison.

Subhuman animals can have or be deprived of circumstantial freedom, even though they do not possess either freedom of choice or moral freedom. Penned up in cages or enclosures, their scope of action is severely limited. They are prevented from carrying out their instinctive impulses or acting in accordance with tendencies that have been acquired through conditioning. Freedom of choice and the freedom to will as one ought are, therefore, not antecedent factors indispensable to freedom of action.

Of these three major forms of freedom or liberty, the only one that needs to be regulated by justice is the third—the circumstantial freedom to do as one pleases. What one wishes to do may be injurious to someone else. It may be an action in violation of a just law. It may be contrary to the best interests of the community of which the individual is a member.

Using the word "license" to designate an illegitimate, unlawful, or unjust exercise of one's circumstantially conferred ability to do as one pleases, doing as one pleases, when so doing is illegitimate, unlawful, or unjust, is not liberty, but license. To think otherwise, or to demand that the scope of one's circumstantial freedom shall be unlimited by such considerations, is to ask for an anarchic liberty, not a freedom that is consonant with living in society cooperatively with other human beings.

Instead of using the word "freedom" for such anarchic liberty —the liberty of an individual in a state of nature rather than of society—let us refer to it as autonomy. Autonomy, as the etymology of that word plainly indicates, consists in being a law unto oneself.

Only an absolute sovereign has autonomy—obeys himself alone, submits to no law made by others, recognizes no authority to regulate his conduct. Autonomy can be possessed only by individuals living completely solitary lives, not by them as members of organized societies that cannot endure or prosper without effective government or coercively enforceable laws.

Since individual human beings do not lead completely solitary lives, since they have never existed, at least not for long, in the so-called state of nature that is more accurately referred to as a state of anarchy, the only autonomy to be found in the world is that possessed by sovereign princes or states. The consequences of such autonomy, as we so well know to our distress, is a state of war—the cold war that is the opposite of peaceful coexistence even when it does not issue in military action.

Living in organized societies under effective government and enforceable laws, as they must in order to survive and prosper, human beings neither have autonomy nor are they entitled to unlimited liberty of action. Autonomy is incompatible with organized society. Unlimited liberty is destructive of it.

It is for this reason that the distinction between liberty and license cannot be dismissed or disregarded. When that distinction is understood and accepted, it follows that the individual who is prevented from doing what he pleases by just restraints suffers no loss of liberty.

The distinction between liberty and license, together with the distinction between anarchic autonomy and freedom in organized society under law and government, leads us to a fourth kind of liberty that is a special variety of circumstantial freedom.

Political liberty, though it is conferred upon the individual by favorable circumstances, is not, like the main form of circumstantial freedom, a freedom to do as one pleases within the constraints of justice. It is instead the liberty that individuals possess when, as fully fledged, enfranchised citizens of a republic, living under constitutional government, their suffrage gives them a voice in the making of the laws under which they live. They are not subject to the arbitrary will of a despot.

While not autonomous, they are self-governing to the extent that they are participants in government. The citizens of a republic are not sovereigns, but each has, in the words of Rousseau, a share in the sovereignty. Constitutional government, said Aristotle, is that form of government in which the citizens are free men and equals, ruling and being ruled in turn.

Slaves do not have political liberty. They are ruled tyrannically in the interest of their masters, not for their own good. The subjects of an absolute monarch do not have political liberty. Even when the absolute despotism under which they live is benevolent, and they are ruled to some extent for their own good, they are ruled as very young children are governed in the household—without a voice in their own government and without participation in the making of the decisions that govern their lives. In a republic, living under constitutional government, those who are deprived of suffrage, for whatever reason, are subjects rather than citizens. They, too, are deprived of political liberty by being disfranchised members of the society in which they live.

Being granted and being denied suffrage constitute the favorable and unfavorable circumstances that confer political liberty upon individuals or deprive them of it. With regard to the main form of circumstantial freedom, which consists in being able, within limits, to do as one pleases, the favorable and unfavorable circumstantial factors are of a different sort.

The unfavorable factors are coercion, constraint, and duress. An individual is not free to do as he pleases when he is constrained by the application of physical force, nor is he free to do as he pleases when he is physically coerced into doing the opposite.

Duress consists in the threat of physical constraint or coercion. The individual who acts contrary to his wishes under a pointed gun is responding to a threat, but the effect is the same as physical coercion. Duress may take other forms. The individual who does the opposite of what he wishes in order to avoid the undesirable consequences of the desired action suffers a loss of freedom from duress.

Circumstances that confer enabling means upon individuals also give them the freedom to do what they wish. Sufficient wealth enables me to dine at the Ritz if I wish to. Deprived of such enabling means, the poor man is not free to dine at the Ritz if he wishes. Without the enabling means provided by scholarships or public funds, the poor in prior centuries were not free to go to colleges or universities if they wished to.

The circumstantial freedom to do as one pleases, within limits, is thus seen to be a freedom *from* coercion, constraint, and duress and a freedom *to* act as one wishes that is provided by enabling means. It is not, however, a freedom *from* having one's conduct regulated by the prescriptions and proscriptions of law.

The sphere of circumstantial liberty is not, as John Stuart Mill wrongly supposed, the sphere of conduct unregulated by law, with the consequence, in Mill's view, that the more our conduct is regulated by law, the less freedom we have. Nor is it true, as Thomas Jefferson said, that the less government the better, because the less government, the freer we are.

An earlier English philosopher, John Locke, provides us with a sounder view of the matter. In the first place, much of our conduct is not and cannot be regulated by law, no matter how massive such regulation may be. This is true not only of the civil law, the positive law of the state, but also of the moral law; for much of our conduct is morally indifferent, neither prescribed nor proscribed by moral rules. In this area where, in Locke's words, "the law prescribes not," we are quite free to do as we please.

Where our conduct does fall under the commands or prohibitions of law, either the civil or the moral law, the virtuous man is still able to do as he pleases, since he pleases to do what he ought. A right rule of conduct and a just civil law command actions that ought to be performed and prohibit acts that ought not to be done.

The morally virtuous individual is one who, having the moral freedom of being able to will and choose as he ought, does voluntarily and freely what the law commands and refrains voluntarily and freely from doing what the law prohibits. He does not suffer restraint from the coercive force of law; he does not act under duress from the threat of coercion.

As Aristotle said, the virtuous man does freely what the criminal does only from fear of the law—fear of its coercive force and of the punishment that may result from violating the law. The criminal, however, does not suffer any loss of liberty when he refrains from breaking the law, for what he wishes to do, being unlawful and unjust, is something he ought not to do anyway, even if he were not constrained by law. His license to do as he wishes, not his liberty, has been taken away.

This leads us to a further point about the relation of law to liberty. Not only is it the case that we are not deprived of liberty by just laws or morally sound rules of conduct. It is also the case that the laws of the state, when they are just, apply coercive force and constraints to secure us from infringements upon our freedom by other individuals who would use illegitimate or unlawful force to interfere with it. Where just laws do not exist or where they are not effectively enforced, individuals are subject to all sorts of depredations and invasions that diminish their freedom.

When just laws are enforced, they enlarge the liberty of the individual. Quite contrary is the condition of persons living under the tyranny of unjust laws, the rule of might rather than of right. Compelled by coercive force or by duress to act neither as they please nor as they ought, their freedom is severely limited. What they have lost by such limitation is true liberty, not license.

The maximization of our circumstantial freedom to do as we

please is the great and real good conferred upon human beings by just laws, effectively enforced. That good is further enhanced by just government, which confers political liberty upon all who are entitled to be enfranchised and to become self-governing through exercising their suffrage.

We have seen why it can be truly said that the virtuous man suffers no loss of freedom when he obeys just laws. It can also be truly said that the citizen who, exercising his suffrage, finds himself in the minority on an important political issue has not ceased to be self-governing and politically free.

The constitution to which the citizen has given consent by exercising his suffrage provides for a decision by the vote of the majority. He has accepted the principle of majority rule and, having done so, the citizen has also accepted, in advance, the result of majority rule, whether or not the voting places him in the majority or in an adversely affected minority.

He may not like the law or policy that the majority has instituted or adopted. Conforming to it may be contrary to his wishes, but when members of a minority do conform to it, they do so without any loss of political liberty. If the law or policy is just, however contrary to their individual interest or judgment it may be, their compliance with it does not deprive them of any freedom at all.

CHAPTER 20

The Liberties to Which We Are Entitled

THERE WOULD BE NO SENSE AT ALL in saying that we are entitled to have a free will or freedom of choice. That is a good conferred on us by nature—or by God. The lower animals are deprived of it, but we cannot say that they are deprived of something they are entitled to.

It would be equally devoid of sense to say that we are entitled to the moral freedom that consists in being able to will as we ought and to refrain from willing as we ought not. We either acquire or fail to acquire such freedom through choices we have ourselves freely made. It is entirely within our power to form or fail to form the virtuous disposition to will as one ought that constitutes an individual's moral freedom. No other human being, and certainly no organized society, can confer such liberty on us or withhold it from us.

According to Christian dogmas concerning man's original sin and man's redemption through Christ's saving grace, fallen man cannot, without God's help, acquire the moral virtue required for moral liberty. That is why Christian theologians refer to moral freedom as the God-given liberty enjoyed only by those whom God has elected for salvation.

On the secular plane of our social lives, it remains the case that we can make no rightful claim upon others or upon society to grant us a freedom that is entirely within our power to possess or lack.

The only liberties to which we can make a claim upon society are the freedom to do as we please within the limits imposed by justice and that variant of circumstantial freedom that is the political liberty enjoyed by enfranchised citizens of a republic.

Whether we have political liberty or not and the extent to which we have a limited freedom to do as we please depend largely, if not entirely, on the society in which we live—its institutions and arrangements, its form of government and its laws.

This being the case, two questions confront us. The first is, Why are we entitled to a limited freedom to do as we wish? Why do we have a right to it? The second question is, Why are we entitled to political liberty? Who has a right to it—every human being or only some?

Answering these questions requires us to discover the basis of entitlements that take the form of natural rights—rights we can demand that a just society should secure for us because they are rights inherent in our human nature, unalienable in the sense that a legal deprivation of them must be justified by special considerations.

Our understanding of the things that are really good for a human being because they fulfill needs that are inherent in human nature provides us with the basis we are looking for.

We are under the moral obligation to pursue happiness, which means trying to make good human lives for ourselves by seeking whatever, corresponding to our natural needs, is really good for us. We have a right to whatever we need to lead good human lives.

Our natural needs provide the basis not only for distinguishing between real and merely apparent goods, but also for distinguishing between the real goods to which we have a natural right and the apparent goods to which we do not have a natural right, but to the acquirement of which we may be privileged on condition that our seeking them does not interfere with anyone else's acquirement of real goods.

Real goods are those to which we have a natural right, not merely a privileged possession. We cannot fulfill our moral obligation to pursue happiness by making a good life for ourselves unless we can make a rightful claim upon society to confer on us the real goods that we need for a good life. Some of these are not entirely within our own power to acquire, because they are, in part at least, goods of fortune, bestowed by beneficent external circumstances.

Thomas Jefferson's too brief and, therefore, too elliptical statement of this truth in the Declaration of Independence yields its full significance only when rephrased and expanded. We are endowed with certain unalienable rights, he wrote, and we are all equally endowed with them because we are by nature equal. Among these are life, liberty, and the pursuit of happiness, which are secured only by just governments and just laws.

The unalienable and natural right to life consists in our entitlement to all the economic goods that we need to sustain life, for without life we cannot live well. Beyond the economic goods indispensable to sustaining life itself are economic goods that we need to live well, above the level of mere subsistence, such as ample time for the pursuits of leisure.

Other things that we need to live well, not mentioned in the Declaration, are health and knowledge. We need them as much as we need a moderate possession of wealth in the form of economic goods, not just to live but to live well. To some extent these goods are within our power to obtain for ourselves; but to the extent that they are not entirely within our power to obtain, we have a right to the help that organized society can provide for obtaining them. That help comes in the form of whatever may be instrumental in obtaining them, such as schooling in the case of knowledge and a healthful environment in the case of health.

How about the right to liberty, a good that is mentioned in the Declaration as one of the principal goods to which we have a right because it is indispensable to our pursuit of happiness —to our living well?

To answer this question, let us first consider liberty of action —the freedom, within limits, to do as we wish. Our natural right to such freedom flows from our natural possession of a free will and a power of free choice, which we exercise in making the decisions that we must make, either rightly or wrongly, in our pursuit of happiness.

What good would it do us to make decisions that we cannot carry out? Without liberty of action, our freedom of choice would be rendered totally ineffective. We would be exercising it without achieving the ultimate good we are under an obligation to seek, if our freedom of choice is thwarted by unjust limitations on our liberty of action, or is nullified by the deprivation of such freedom. Lacking free will and freedom of choice, the lower animals have no rightful claim on liberty of action. Zoos do not exist in violation of rights. However much we may sympathize with caged or confined animals, we are not moved by a sense of injustice done to them.

We feel differently about Epictetus in chains and Boethius in prison. They could exercise their freedom of choice to will as they ought and so they enjoyed the moral freedom that is the prize of virtuous human beings. But virtuous human beings are not always able to lead good human lives. Moral virtue alone is not sufficient. Good fortune, in the form of beneficent external circumstances, is also indispensable to the successful pursuit of happiness.

Man's natural freedom of choice and his obligation to make

a good life for himself by making right choices is the basis of his entitlement by natural right to liberty of action. What about his entitlement to that variant of circumstantial freedom that is political liberty?

The reasoning here runs parallel to that in which we have just engaged. Again, human nature provides the answer. But here, in place of man's natural freedom of choice as the basis of the entitlement to liberty of action, is man's nature as a political animal.

To be a political animal involves more than being the kind of social animal that bees, ants, wasps, wolves, and other gregarious organisms are. Social or gregarious animals need to live in association with others of their kind. Man, too, is a social or gregarious animal in this sense. He naturally needs to live in association with other human beings in organized societies.

Unlike the organized societies of the social insects, which are entirely determined by the instincts of the species, human societies are voluntarily formed and conventionally instituted. They are natural societies only in the sense that man, being gregarious, needs to live in association with other human beings. They are at the same time conventional in the sense that the shape they take—the forms of government, the laws, the institutions, and other arrangements that constitute their organization—are products of rational and free, not instinctive, determination.

A political community is a society that is thus constituted. To say that man is by nature a political as well as a social animal is to say that he is by nature inclined to live in political communities and to participate in political activity—to be a self-governing citizen in a republic.

In short, being political by nature means that man by nature needs political liberty—the freedom of an enfranchised citizen —in order to live humanly well. This is the basis of man's entitlement, by natural right, to political liberty.

Deprived of political liberty, as slaves are or as are the subjects of a despot no matter how benevolent, human beings cannot fulfill all their natural propensities and lead fully human lives. They are deprived of a real good to which they are by nature entitled. The same is true of those who, living under constitutional governments or in republics, are nevertheless disfranchised and thus deprived of political liberty.

Are there any grounds to justify the disfranchisement of human beings who are by nature political animals? Only two: infancy and pathological disablement by amentia or dementia —by a degree of feeblemindedness or of insanity that calls for hospitalization and medical care.

In addition, criminal behavior justifies a deprivation of political liberty, as well as liberty of action, either for a period of time or for life. The criminal, by his own behavior, has himself forfeited the exercise of a right that is unalienably his as a human being. The exercise of that right, temporarily in abeyance, is restored in full measure when he has served his term, if that is anything short of life.

CHAPTER 21

The Dimensions of Equality

TWO THINGS ARE EQUAL when one is neither more nor less than
the other in an identified respect. When they are unequal, their
inequality consists in one being more, the other less—one superior, the other inferior—in some respect.

This understanding of equality and inequality remains constant in all the dimensions in which things are related as equal
or unequal. What differs as one distinguishes different dimensions is (1) the character of the subjects of which equality and
inequality are predicated, (2) the mode of the predication, and
(3) the qualifications attached to the predication. Let us consider each of these differences in turn.

1. Personal and Circumstantial Equality

The subjects being compared and regarded as equal or unequal fall into two main categories: human beings and every-

thing else—all the external circumstances under which human beings live and act and whatever factors impinge upon their conduct and their welfare. I shall refer to the first category as human or personal equality and inequality, and to the second as circumstantial equality and inequality.

Human equality and inequality can be further subdivided into that which arises from the endowments that persons bring into this world at birth and that which derives from their attainments—the attributes or characteristics they acquire in the course of their lives, the degree to which they develop their innate endowments, and the work of their hands and minds.

Inequality in height exemplifies a human inequality that is genetically determined and so is an inequality between two persons that is a matter of native endowment. To whatever extent we are born with one or another degree of intelligence, human equality and inequality in this respect are also a matter of native endowment.

Two human beings who start out equal in their genetically determined degree of intelligence may develop that endowment to different degrees, either through what they themselves do with their minds or because of the circumstances under which they are reared, trained, and educated. In either case, they may end up unequal in their mental attainments. One may know more than the other or have more skill in the use of his mind.

Two persons born with the same capacity for engaging in a certain sport may, at a later stage in their lives, be unequal in the degree of their acquired skill in playing tennis or in swimming.

One individual may put his native endowments to work in the production of wealth or other goods, while another, with equal endowments, may squander his talents, producing nothing, or employ them less assiduously and efficiently, producing less. They must then be regarded as unequal in this respect.

The personal equality or inequality that stems from the degree to which individuals are natively endowed in one way or another, let us call natural, as contrasted with the equality or inequality of human attainments, which can be referred to as acquired. All personal equalities and inequalities are either natural or acquired.

When we turn from human equality and inequality, natural or acquired, to circumstantial equality and inequality, we confront the difference between the type of circumstantial equality or inequality that has come to be called equality or inequality of condition, and the type that has come to be called equality or inequality of opportunity.

The difference between equality of condition and equality of opportunity can best be illustrated by a race in which individuals all start out with no one affected by circumstances more or less favorable to winning the race. Their equality of opportunity consists in an equality in the initial conditions under which they enter the race. When the race is run, these same individuals end up unequal. According to the speed with which they ran the race, one comes in first, another second, another third, and so on. If prizes are awarded, the gold, silver, and bronze medals represent an inequality of conditions, which is also sometimes called an inequality of results.

The example I have used is complicated by the fact that the runners who enjoy an equality of opportunity with regard to external circumstances may enter the race unequal in their native endowments as competitors. Even if they are equal in their native endowments, they may enter the race unequal in the degree to which they, by exercise and training, have developed those endowments. Prior inequalities of endowment or attainment will, of course, affect the inequality of resulting conditions in spite of the equality of opportunity provided by the equal initial conditions under which they entered the race.

That is why it is often pointed out that if human beings are granted nothing more than equality of opportunity, inequality of conditions is likely to result. The individuals who are better endowed or better trained are most likely to end up ahead of those less well endowed or trained.

An equality of resulting conditions that is unaffected by equality of opportunity (enjoyed by individuals of unequal endowment and attainment) may be achievable only by strenuous efforts on the part of society to see that its individual members are somehow given or granted such equality. When, for example, all members of a society—or all with justifiable exceptions—are given the same political status, let us say that of citizenship with suffrage, an equality of political condition results.

Equality before the law is another example of an equality of condition that a society can establish. It does so when it accords equal treatment in the courts and in other aspects of the legal process to all individuals regardless of their inequalities of endowment or attainment, regardless whether they are rich or poor, regardless of the ethnic group to which they belong, and so on. Such equality of treatment does not discriminate in any way among persons who differ from one another in a wide variety of respects that are irrelevant to the treatment they should receive in the legal process.

Equality of condition may be either an equality in the status granted individuals, an equality in the treatment accorded them, or an equality with respect to their possession of one or another basic human good, such as political liberty, wealth, a healthful environment, or schooling. Their equal possession of such goods depends upon factors controlled by society, not entirely by themselves.

For our present purposes, it will suffice to subdivide equality or inequality of conditions into three main categories: political, economic, and social. Equality of opportunity (which is an equality of initial as opposed to resulting condition) can be similarly subdivided.

2. *Equality That Does Exist and Equality That Ought to Exist*

When we predicate equality or inequality of persons or conditions, the predication may be either declarative or prescriptive. To say that two individuals *are* or *are not* equal in a certain respect is declarative. To say that they *should* or *ought to* be equal or unequal in a certain respect is prescriptive.

In the sphere of human equality and inequality, prescriptive statements make no sense. We cannot say that human beings ought to be equal or unequal in any personal respect, neither with regard to their endowments nor with regard to their attainments. All that we can meaningfully say, as a matter of fact, is that they *are* personally equal in this respect and unequal in that respect.

It has been suggested that individuals, entering into association with one another to form a community, *should* do so on a supposition contrary to fact; namely, that they are all personally equal in every important respect. This contrafactual supposition is defended on the ground that organized society can come into existence on the basis of a social contract only if all who enter into that contract suppose themselves to be completely equal. If a veil of ignorance about the facts, which permits them to make this contrafactual supposition, were not operative, it is thought that they would not agree to become participants in the social contract.

The social contract is a myth that can be dismissed as unnecessary for the explanation of the origin of political communities. With it goes the veil of ignorance that is thought necessary for the formation of society by means of a social contract. There is no sense in saying that human beings *ought* to regard themselves as personally equal in all important respects when they know the facts to be quite the contrary. Human communities of all sorts, including states or civil societies, have come into existence and have been formed by individuals who enter into such associations in spite of their well-known and acknowledged personal inequalities in many important respects.

Turning from personal to circumstantial equality and inequality, we find that both declarative and prescriptive statements can be made with good sense. We can say that this group of individuals *are* or *are not* equal with respect to a given circumstance affecting their lives; or we can say that they *ought* or *ought not* to be equal in that respect.

For example, those who, living under a constitutional government, are accorded the status of citizenship have an equality of status. They are all equal in their possession of the political liberty attendant upon that status. However, some members of that society may not be accorded the status of citizenship with suffrage. Then, as a matter of fact, the enfranchised and the disfranchised members of the society will be politically unequal —unequal in political status and unequal with respect to political liberty.

When this is factually the case, conflicting prescriptive proposals may be advanced. Exponents of the democratic principle of universal suffrage may argue that all persons in a republic (or all with few justifiable exceptions) *should* be enfranchised. Opponents of universal suffrage, for one reason or another, may argue that the franchise *should* be restricted to persons having this or that special qualification, such as gender, skin color, or amount of property possessed.

Justice enters into the picture as regulative only in the sphere of circumstantial equality and inequality, because only there can we make prescriptive proposals.

Considerations of justice do not enter in the sphere of human equality and inequality where only declarative statements can be made and prescriptive proposals are impossible. Personal equality or inequality, natural or acquired, is neither just nor unjust. It is simply a matter of fact.

It is pointless to say that if nature were just, human beings would be born equal in all important respects. Nature is neither just nor unjust in the gifts it bestows. Only human beings can be just or unjust in the proposals they advance with regard to an equality of conditions or with regard to an inequality of results.

Where an inequality of conditions exists but ought not to prevail, justice may call for rectifying this by establishing an equality of conditions in its place. With regard to individuals who make unequal contributions by the work they do or the goods they produce, justice may call for an inequality of results in the rewards they receive.

3. Equality in Kind and Inequality in Degree

We come finally to the most difficult and at the same time the most important qualification or distinction to be considered in our statements about equality, whether declarative or prescriptive. It consists in the distinction between (a) an equality of conditions that exists or ought to exist without any attendant difference in degree and (b) an equality of conditions that exists or ought to exist but which is accompanied by differences in degree and so by inequalities among those who are equal in a given respect.

The following example may make this clear. All who have the status of citizenship with suffrage are equal in their political condition and with respect to their possession of political liberty. But when the members of a society are divided into the enfranchised and the disfranchised, an inequality of political conditions exists. If that is unjust, it can be rectified by establishing universal suffrage.

When, with universal suffrage, all enjoy an equality of political status, it may still remain the case that some citizens elected or appointed to public office exercise a greater degree of political power than citizens who are not public officials. They are able to participate in the affairs of government to a higher degree than ordinary citizens. Here, then, we have an equality of condition that is accompanied by differences in degree and so by inequality.

All who are citizens have some degree of political power, since all through suffrage can participate in the affairs of government. But some citizens, through exercising the power vested in certain public offices, have more political power than others.

Now let us consider a republic in which the suffrage is restricted rather than universal. There the population will, first of all, be divided into two politically unequal segments—(a) those who have the status of citizenship with suffrage and, consequently, political liberty and some degree of political power, and (b) those who do not have the status in question, and so have no political liberty and no degree of political power.

There will be a second source of political inequality in the society we are considering. This time the political inequality will occur only among those who are politically equal. Equal because they all have suffrage, the enfranchised portion of the population will consist of persons who are unequal in the degree of political power they possess. As citizens with suffrage, all will have some degree of political power, but some who have it will have more of it, and some less.

The distinction that confronts us here can be summarized by saying that, in the sphere of circumstantial equality, equality prevails among those who *have* a certain condition, and inequality prevails between the group that *has it* and the group that *does not have it*. This is an equality among all the haves and an inequality between the haves and the have-nots. In addition, among the haves, there may be differences in the degree to which they possess and enjoy the condition in question, some having more of it, some less. Here we are looking at an attendant inequality among the haves, one that exists between the individual who *has more* and the individual who *has less*.

It is difficult to name the equality and inequality we have been considering. I propose to call the equality that prevails among haves an equality in kind, and the inequality between haves and have-nots an inequality in kind. In contradistinction, I propose to call the inequality among the haves, according as one has more and one has less, an inequality in degree.

If all persons are equal in their having the same specific human nature and, with that, the same species-specific properties, that is an equality in kind. But one person may be endowed with a specific property to a higher degree than another. The resultant personal inequality of human beings, all members of the same species but differing from one another as individuals, is an inequality in degree.

In the sphere of circumstantial equality, both types of equality may prevail in fact. All members of a society may be equal in kind as haves in a certain respect, but they may also be unequal in degree, one being a have-more, another a have-less. It is also possible, though very unlikely, that, as a matter of fact, all may be equal in kind as haves without any accompanying difference in degree.

Those who would rectify the injustice of existent inequalities of condition differ radically in the proposals they advance.

There are those who would defend the prescriptive judgment that, with respect to certain conditions, political, economic, or social, all *should* be equal in kind without any attendant inequality in degree. All ought to be haves with respect to this or that important human good, but among the haves, none should have more and none have less.

Opposed to them are those who would defend the prescriptive judgment that, with respect to the same conditions, all *should* be equal in kind, adding that such equality in kind *should* be attended by inequalities in degree. While all ought to be haves with respect to the human goods in question, some ought to have more, and some less.

Which of these two conflicting views is the correct view of what justice requires with respect to circumstantial equality— equality of status, treatment, possessions, and opportunity—is the question I shall attempt to answer in the following chapter. In closing this chapter, I cannot refrain from expressing my sympathy for readers who have struggled to read it carefully. I know they have found the treatment of equality difficult, more difficult than the treatment of liberty. I find it so myself. Though both are complex ideas, each embracing a diversity of modes, the dimensions of equality are a much more complex subject than are the kinds of liberty.

CHAPTER 22

The Equalities to Which
We Are Entitled

THIS CHAPTER, AS ITS TITLE INDICATES, runs parallel to Chapter 20. There we were concerned with the liberties to which we are entitled; here with the equalities that we have a right to—the equalities that justice requires.

The parallelism should enable readers to surmise at once the basis for our entitlement to certain equalities. Just as with the liberties to which we have a natural right, so here with respect to the equalities that we can rightfully claim, the ultimate basis of the right lies in the nature of man.

If human beings were not by nature endowed with freedom of the will and the power of free choice, to be exercised in the pursuit of the ultimate good that they are morally obliged to seek, they would not have, by nature, a right to liberty of action. If they were not by nature political animals, they would not have by nature the right to political liberty. Their right to these liberties lies in the fact that deprivation of them renders their power of free choice ineffective in the pursuit of happiness and frustrates their natural inclination to participate in political affairs.

The equalities to which we are all entitled, by virtue of being human, are circumstantial, not personal. They are equalities of condition—of status, treatment, and opportunity. How does our humanity justify our right to these equalities?

The answer is that, by being human, we are all equal—equal as persons, equal in our humanity. One individual cannot be more or less human than another, more or less of a person. The dignity we attribute to being a person rather than a thing is not subject to differences in degree. The equality of all human beings is the equality of their dignity as persons.

Were all human beings not equal in their common humanity, did they not all equally have the dignity of persons, they would not all be entitled to equalities of condition. The point is strikingly illustrated by an ancient and erroneous doctrine (which, by the way, takes many disguised forms in the modern world) that some human beings are *by nature* slaves and so are radically inferior to other human beings who are *by nature* their masters. If this view of the facts were correct, as it is not, all human beings would *not* be entitled to any equality of condition—equality of status, treatment, and opportunity.

The factual basis for the correct view is biological. All members of any biological species, human or otherwise, are alike in possessing the properties or powers that are genetically determined attributes of that species of living organism. These common properties, shared by all individuals of a certain species, are appropriately called species-specific.

Of these species-specific properties, some are generic, shared by other animals; such, for example, in the case of human beings, are their vegetative and sensitive powers. Only some of man's species-specific properties consist of powers that are not generic, but being distinctive and definitive of the human species, differentiate human beings as different in kind from other animals.

To say that all human beings are equal in their common humanity is, therefore, to say that all have the same species-specific properties, both those that are generic properties shared by other animals and those that are distinctive and definitive of the human species, such as man's power of free choice and his power of conceptual thought.

The statement in the Declaration of Independence that all men are created equal and endowed by their Creator with certain unalienable rights is not, on the face of it, self-evidently true. Nor can it be made self-evident by substituting "are by nature equal" for "created equal," and "endowed by nature with certain unalienable rights" for "endowed by their Creator with certain unalienable rights."

The truth of the statement, even when the substitutions are made, is the truth of a conclusion reached by reasoning in the light of factual evidence, evidence and reasoning that refutes the ancient doctrine that some human beings (all members of the same species) are by nature slaves.

I am not going to present here the evidence and expound the reasoning that establishes the truth of the conclusion that all human beings, as members of the species *Homo sapiens,* are *ipso facto* equal. I have done that in another book, entitled *The Difference of Man and the Difference It Makes.*

The conclusion there reached is that man differs in kind, not merely in degree, from other animal organisms, which means that while he has certain generic properties shared by them, with respect to which he may differ in degree from them, human beings also have certain distinctive properties that only they possess and that all other animals totally lack. It is the having and not having of these distinctive human powers that differentiates human beings in kind from other animals.

The truth of the proposition that all human beings are by nature equal is confined to the one respect in which that equality can be truly affirmed; namely, their all being equally human, their having the species-specific properties and especially the differentiating properties that belong to all members of the species.

There is no other respect in which *all* human beings are equal. Two or more individuals may be personally equal in some other respect, such as height, intelligence, talent, or virtue, but equality in such respects is never true of all.

The contrary is true. When we consider all members of the human species, we find that, in every respect other than their possession of the same species-specific properties and powers, inequalities in degree prevail. In other words, though all human beings have the same generic and specifically distinctive properties and powers, some will have them to a higher, some to a lower, degree than others.

Individual members of the species differ from one another either by innate endowment, genetically determined, or by voluntary attainment, individually acquired. From these individual differences arise the inequalities in degree that make one individual superior or inferior to another in some particular respect.

One individual, by nature equal to another in kind, which means equal through having the same species-specific properties, may be by nature unequal to another in degree, which means being genetically endowed with a higher or lower degree—with more or less—of the properties or powers that both possess at birth. In addition, one may be superior or inferior to another in individually acquired attainments as well as in genetically determined endowments. This may wholly result from differences in individual effort; but it may also be partly due to the favorable or unfavorable circumstances under which the individual strives to accomplish something.

For brevity of reference, let us use the phrase "specific equality" to refer to the personal equality in kind that is the one equality possessed by all human beings. Let us use the phrase "individual equality" or "individual inequality" to refer to the personal equality and inequality of human beings in all other respects, whether that be equality and inequality in degree of endowments or equality and inequality in degree of attainments.

From the declarative statement about the specific equality in kind of all human beings, what prescription follows? The answer is that all human beings are in justice or by right entitled to a circumstantial equality in kind, especially with respect to political status, treatment, and opportunity and with respect to economic status, treatment, and opportunity.

Being by nature equal, they are all endowed by nature with certain unalienable rights, unalienable because they are inherent in man's specific nature, not merely bestowed upon man by legal enactment. Legal enactment may be necessary to secure these rights, but it does not constitute their unalienability.

Merely legal rights are alienable. Being granted by the state, they can be taken away by the state. Natural rights can be secured or violated by the state, but they do not come into existence through being granted by the state; nor does their existence cease when they are not acknowledged or secured by the laws of the state.

As we have seen, human beings, having by nature the power of free choice, have a natural and unalienable right to liberty of action. Being also by nature political animals, they have a natural and unalienable right to political liberty and participation. Justice requires that all should be accorded the equal status of citizenship with suffrage, through which status they can exercise their power to participate in government. All citizens have this power. It is totally lacking in those who, being disfranchised, are deprived of it. Having this power to some degree confers upon all citizens with suffrage a circumstantial equality in kind. Between those who have it and those who are deprived of it, there is a circumstantial inequality in kind.

Turning now from the political to the economic sphere, parallel reasoning reaches a parallel conclusion. Both as an animal generically, and as a specifically human animal, man has certain biological needs, such as his need for the means of subsistence in order to survive, and his need for certain comforts and conveniences of life, which he needs to live humanly well. Economic goods are the goods that man by nature needs in order to survive and, beyond that, to live well—to engage successfully in the pursuit of happiness.

These include more than food and drink, clothing and shelter. They include schooling as instrumental to fulfilling man's need for knowledge and skill; a healthful environment as instrumental to fulfilling man's need for health; ample free time from toil or earning a living as instrumental to fulfilling man's need to engage in play for the pleasure of it and in the pursuits of leisure for the improvement of his mind by engagement in all forms of learning and creative activity.

From these natural needs for the goods mentioned and for the goods that are instrumental to achieving them arises man's natural right to the possession of that *sufficiency* of economic goods which is *enough* for living well—for making a good life. The existence of natural right leads us to the conclusion that every human being is entitled to whatever economic goods any human being needs to lead a good life.

Just as all human beings are entitled to a political equality in kind, so they are all entitled to an economic equality in kind.

All should be haves with respect to political liberty, none have-nots, none disfranchised persons totally deprived of the power of political participation that a political animal needs.

All should be haves with respect to wealth in the form of whatever economic goods a human being needs to live well, at least that sufficiency of such goods which is enough for the purpose. None can be have-nots in the sense of being totally deprived of such goods, for total deprivation means death. But none should be destitute—have-nots in the sense of being deprived of enough wealth to live well.

In both the political and economic sphere, justice requires only as much equality of conditions as human beings have a natural right to on the basis of their natural needs. The state-

ment of the matter just made occupies a middle position between the two extremist views mentioned earlier.

At one extreme, the libertarian maintains that the only circumstantial equality to which all human beings are entitled is
equality of opportunity. He argues for this view on the ground
that such equality tends to maximize individual liberty of action, especially freedom of enterprise in the economic sphere.

The libertarian rightly thinks that attempts on the part of
organized society to establish an equality of economic condition other than an equality of opportunity will inevitably result
in government regulations and interferences in economic activities that restrict individual liberty of action and put curbs on
freedom of enterprise. Where he is wrong is in failing to see
that such curtailments of freedom, made in the interests of justice, are proper limitations of liberty. His error lies in asking
for more liberty than justice allows.

At the opposite extreme, the egalitarian maintains that the
circumstantial equality to which all human beings are entitled
should not be merely an equality in kind that is accompanied
by inequalities in degree. It should be more than that. It should
be the extreme form of circumstantial equality, which is an
equality of condition attended by no inequalities in degree.

Stated in political terms, this would mean that all should be
haves in the sense of having political liberty and power, but no
individual should have more, and none less, of the power that
all should have because it is requisite for participation in political life.

Stated in economic terms, this would mean that all should be
haves with respect to wealth in the form of the economic goods
needed to live humanly well, but also that all should have the
same amount of wealth. None should have more, and none
less, of the wealth that everyone needs for the successful pursuit of happiness.

The middle position between these erroneous extremes, in
both the political and the economic spheres, calls for a moderate, not an extreme, form of circumstantial equality. With re-

gard to the possession of political or economic goods, real goods that every human being needs, it calls for no more than everyone is entitled to by natural right. It is willing to settle for no less.

A moderate or justly limited equality of conditions is an equality in kind, with respect to either political or economic goods, but one that is accompanied by inequalities in degree that justice also requires. Justice requires only that all shall be haves. It does not require that all shall be haves *to the same degree*. On the contrary, as the next chapter will attempt to make clear, some are entitled by justice to more, and some to less, of the goods that everyone is entitled by justice to have.

Two additional reasons can be given for rejecting the wrong prescription concerning equality of conditions that the egalitarian recommends on the basis of man's specific personal equality.

First of all, he appears to forget that the specific equality of all members of the human species is accompanied by individual inequalities of all sorts, both in endowments and attainments and in what use individuals make of their endowments and attainments.

Human individuals are not all equal in the way that so many precision-made ball bearings are alike—identical with one another in every respect except number, all having the same properties without any difference in degree. Unlike the ball bearings, which of course have no individuality at all, human individuality consists of individual differences that result in one person's having more or less of the same attributes that also belong to another.

To recommend the prescription that all human beings are entitled to a circumstantial equality of conditions, political and economic, that should involve no differences in degree is to neglect or overlook the existence of significant individual inequalities in degree among human beings. These personal inequalities in degree call for circumstantial inequalities in degree, just as our personal equality in kind calls for circumstantial equality in kind.

The error being made by the egalitarian arises in the same way as the one made by the elitist who neglects or overlooks the personal equality in kind of all human beings. On the sole basis of personal inequalities in degree, the elitist recommends circumstantial inequality in degree with respect to political and economic goods. He rejects the recommendation of any circumstantial equality in kind, except perhaps equality of opportunity. The elitist makes that one exception because he believes that, in the race of life, the superior will win.

Elitism can be avoided without going to the opposite extreme of egalitarianism, simply by rendering what is in justice due human beings by reference to their personal equality without overlooking their individual inequalities and by reference to their individual inequalities without ignoring their personal equality. In recent history, the most glaring and egregious example of an egalitarian overreaction against elitism is provided by the cultural revolution to which China was subjected under the gang of four.

A second reason for rejecting the extremism of the egalitarian looks not to its injustice, but to its practical unfeasibility.

It is possible for miscarriages of justice to occur that would permit liberty to run rampant beyond limits and to become injurious license. The libertarian extreme is feasible, but not the egalitarian extreme. More liberty than justice allows is possible in society, but more equality than justice requires cannot be sustained.

To recommend that all should be haves with respect to political liberty and power, but that none should have more and none less, is to recommend a form of direct democracy so extreme that it would allow no distinction whatsoever between citizens in or out of public office—a democracy in which there are no magistrates, one in which everything is decided directly by a majority vote of the whole citizenry.

It is doubtful whether such extreme democracy ever existed,

in Athens or in New England townships. It certainly would not be practically feasible in any state of considerable size; having a population so large that all its members could not deal with each other face to face, nor when confronted with the complexity of problems that states and governments must deal with in the contemporary world.

In the economic sphere, to recommend that all should be haves with respect to wealth in the form of whatever economic goods human beings need to live well, but that none should be richer and none poorer in their possession of wealth, is to recommend an equality of conditions that has never existed, except perhaps in monasteries where the monks, taking the vow of poverty, participate equally in what wealth is available for the community as a whole.

If, under secular conditions, all individuals or all families were somehow to come into possession of the same amount of wealth, in whatever form, that absolute equality of economic condition would not last for long. A magic wand would be needed, not only to bring it into existence, but also to make it endure. No one has ever worked out a plan whereby, short of magic, this extreme form of economic equality might become feasible.

CHAPTER 23

The Inequalities That Justice Also Requires

WE ARE HERE CONCERNED with political and economic equalities that are equalities in kind to which differences in degree must be added. The resultant inequalities in degree occur among those who are already equal in kind.

Those who are all haves, either politically or economically, will then include those who have more and those who have less, with no one having less than is needed for the purpose and no one having more than is compatible with everyone having enough.

Let me illustrate this with regard to political equality. That will help us to deal with the more difficult case of economic equality.

Entitled to have, through citizenship with suffrage, the minimal measure of political liberty and power attendant upon that status, some citizens deserve, in varying degrees, more power to participate in the affairs of government. The citizens in question happen for a time to hold one or another public office and are thereby charged with the responsibility to perform functions constitutionally assigned to such offices. In proportion to their responsibilities, it is right and fit that they should have more political power and a greater voice in public affairs.

The minimal measure allotted ordinary citizens, those not in public office, suffices for participation through elections, having a voice in referendums or plebiscites, and engaging in party politics, local or national. That much at least is requisite for the exercise of suffrage. Those who have, in varying degrees, more than this are entitled to it by what they are called upon to do politically over and above discharging the duties of ordinary citizens.

As Alexander Hamilton pointed out, unless political power is proportionate to political responsibility, the responsibility cannot be effectively discharged. Citizens in public office must, therefore, exercise more political power than when they are not in office.

Here, then, in a constitutional government with universal suffrage, all persons, except infants and the pathologically disabled, are politically equal as citizens with suffrage. All have the requisite minimal measure of power for participation in public affairs. Some of them, holding public office, have in varying degrees more power and a greater voice in public affairs. But none has too much, which would be the case only if the chief magistrate or head of state were to arrogate to himself unconstitutional powers that effectively nullified the suffrage of ordinary citizens.

The principle of justice that is operative here differs from the principle that we saw operative with regard to the political equality in kind to which all human beings are by right entitled.

There, the entitlement was based on the personal equality in kind of all human beings and on their endowment with the same natural rights based on needs inherent in human nature, among which is the need and right of a political animal to have a voice in his political affairs.

Here, the justification of giving some citizens more political power and a greater voice in public affairs rests not on what they are as human beings, but upon what they are called upon to do by the offices they hold—on the political functions they have the responsibility of performing.

The justice of rendering to each what is his or hers by natural right is the justice that entitles all to political and economic equality—an equality in kind that puts all, in the first instance, on the base line of having enough of the political and economic goods that they need in order to live well.

The justice of treating equals equally and unequals unequally in proportion to their inequality is the justice that entitles some of the haves to have more and some to have less in varying degrees. Because it is a point of the greatest importance, let me repeat two qualifications: (1) *none less than enough for the purpose and* (2) *none more than is compatible with everyone having enough.*

Accordingly, all enfranchised citizens are equal in kind on the base line, on which they all share the same minimal degree of political power requisite for an effective discharge of their suffrage. Above the base line are some of those same citizens who, while in public office by election or appointment, have more political power in varying degrees.

Those above the base line have more political power *legitimately* (i.e., by just entitlement) only if they have it because of the power constitutionally vested in the office they hold. They have it *illegitimately* if they have it through the undue influence they are able to exercise because of their massive wealth, their social standing in the community, their personal charisma, or some other form of privilege or prestige.

The political picture we have just surveyed provides us with a model to adapt in dealing with economic equality and inequality.

The first principle of justice here as in the political sphere is the principle of rendering to each what belongs to all by natural right. All have a natural right to that sufficiency of economic goods which is enough to provide them with the wealth they need to lead decent human lives, lives not crippled by economic deprivation to a degree that amounts to destitution.

When this first principle of justice is operative in a society without any exceptions, for there are no justifiable exceptions here as there are in the political sphere, then all are haves economically—all are economically equal in kind on the base line, which is determined by that measure or degree of wealth sufficient for the purpose.

More than that is more than enough. Can it be justified? Are some human beings rightly entitled to more wealth than that possessed by those who remain on the base line? Why does justice require the economic inequality in degree that results when some haves have more than others?

The second principle of justice provides the answer to these questions, as it does in the political sphere. But the economic application of that principle is somewhat different.

Those who have more than the minimal measure of wealth that all require for their natural needs are not entitled to it by natural right. Their entitlement derives from what they do, not from what they are as human beings.

In the political sphere, what those entitled to more political power do is to discharge the functions of the political offices they hold, for the performance of which they are constitutionally responsible. In the economic sphere, what those entitled to more wealth do is to make a greater contribution to the production of wealth.

That is certainly the principal, if not the only, way in which they can come into legitimate possession of more wealth. They possess it illegitimately if they come by it through theft, or seizure, or through exercising any influence on the distribution of wealth other than the merit of their productive contribution.

The second principle of justice, as applied in the economic

sphere, can be initially stated as follows: To each the wealth that he produces. This maxim makes sense only in the simple case in which each individual works by himself to produce wealth. In that case, the man who produces more is by right entitled to all that he produces.

When we pass from the simple to the more complex case in which men work together to produce wealth, under a variety of arrangements and by a variety of productive means, the maxim must be reworded as follows: To each in proportion to his contribution to the total wealth that all engage cooperatively in producing.

If all who are engaged cooperatively make equal contributions, which is unlikely in most instances of complex economic operations, then each is entitled to share equally in the distribution of the wealth produced. When, as is more likely, the contributions of those engaged cooperatively are unequal, justice requires that the results shall also be unequal, unequal in proportion to the inequality of contribution.

Those who have made a greater contribution are justly entitled to more wealth than those who contribute less. Two qualifications must be immediately attached to this rule.

First, all, in one way or another, must be equal on the economic base line that is determined by that minimal measure of sufficient wealth to satisfy man's economic needs. To this much everyone has a natural right.

Second, since the amount of wealth available for distribution is limited, no one should be in a position to earn by his productive contribution—to earn, not to steal or seize—so much wealth that not enough remains for distribution, in one way or another, to put all individuals or families on the base line of economic sufficiency.

None, in short, should be rendered destitute by the distribution of wealth in unequal amounts, even if that distribution can be justified by the inequality of individual contributions.

We must observe here a complication in the formulation of economic justice that does not occur in the political sphere. No conflict arises there between (*a*) the just entitlement of all to be political haves (all with that minimal measure of political power requisite for the effective exercise of suffrage), and (*b*) the justice of an unequal distribution of political power, above the base line where all are politically equal, according to the functions those in public office are called upon to perform and the unequal degrees of responsibility involved in the performance of these functions.

No one can have so much political power *legitimately* that the base line itself is destroyed, or that some are in effect disfranchised and dropped below the base line to a position of political subjection or slavery, deprived of all political liberty and power.

In the economic sphere, the situation is different. It is possible for some to acquire *legitimately* so much of the limited supply of wealth that not enough is left for a just distribution to all of the minimal measure—enough wealth to supply what everyone needs to lead a decent human life.

To acknowledge this is to recognize that, in the economic sphere, the first and second principles of justice come into conflict. The first principle, which requires that every individual or family shall have that minimal measure to which all are by natural right entitled, is nullified by the second principle, which awards more wealth to those who contribute more to its production, when some individuals or families are in a position to make so great a contribution that their just award—their legitimate acquirement of a great amount of wealth—is so massive that not enough is left for distribution in accordance with economic needs, which are the same for all.

The conflict between these two principles of justice in the economic sphere can be resolved only by adding a restrictive qualification to the second. The amount of wealth that anyone can justly acquire must be limited so that enough of the finite supply is left for a just distribution in accordance with natural rights. This principle of limitation on an otherwise just acquisition of wealth was first enunciated by John Locke in the chapter on property in his *Second Treatise on Civil Government*.

That those who contribute unequally shall receive unequally in proportion to the inequality of their contribution is a principle of justice that must be made subservient to the principle of justice that calls for an equal distribution to all of that minimal measure of wealth everyone needs. Justice according to natural rights takes precedence in the economic sphere over justice according to the equality or inequality of the contributions made to the production of wealth.

The foregoing analysis of economic justice calls for brief comment on Marxist maxims with regard to the distribution of wealth.

In his *Critique of the Gotha Program,* Karl Marx modified the original Communist maxim for the distribution of wealth—the egalitarian precept "To all alike, an equality without any difference in degree"—by the statement "From each according to his ability; to each according to his needs."

The context makes absolutely clear that Marx did not have in mind the natural needs that are common to all human beings, for then he would not have said "To each according to his needs," but rather "To all alike according to their common human needs." That statement would have introduced no modification of the original egalitarian precept.

What is clear from the context is that Marx had in mind not the natural needs, which are the same for everyone, but those contingent circumstantial needs that result from one worker's being older or younger than another, having a larger family to support than another, or having to take care of some member of his family disabled by illness.

Insofar as these contingent circumstantial needs justify unequal compensation to different workers even if those workers perform the same functions and make equal contributions to the production of wealth, the original egalitarian precept would appear to be superseded by the addition of differences in degree to an equality in kind.

However, it can still be maintained that all are equal in kind, without the addition of differences in degree. The satisfaction of the differential contingent needs still leaves all families having just enough. Enough for one family with more dependents to support or with care of members disabled by illness is neither more nor less than enough for another family with fewer dependents and no illness.

The real modification of the original egalitarian precept was introduced later by Nikita Khrushchev when he added the precept "To each according to his contribution." This did not displace but supplemented the maxim "To each according to his needs"—whether natural or circumstantial.

When the two maxims are combined and conflict between them is resolved by making the second subservient to the first, the result is an economic equality in kind (every individual or family being on the base line of the haves who have enough) modified by an economic inequality in degree (some individuals or families rising above the base line and having more than enough, though never too much with the result that some are rendered destitute).

The maxims of justice with respect to the distribution of political power we all recognize to be the precepts of constitutional democracy. The parallel maxims of justice with respect to the distribution of wealth are the precepts of socialism. Those who shy away from that word, and may even be inclined to reject sound maxims of economic justice because the word "socialism" is attached to them, should realize that socialism is not the same as communism.

The precepts of socialism can be fulfilled in a variety of ways, only one of which may be the communist way, which is the way of state capitalism—the abolition of private ownership of the means of production and the complete control of both the production and the distribution of wealth by the state.

The precepts of socialism can also be fulfilled in the socialized capitalism that is our own mixed economy, in which private ownership of the means of production remains, in which there is both a private and a public sector, in which there is freedom of enterprise regulated by justice, not totally unregulated laissez-faire.

The only kind of economy in which the precepts of socialism cannot be fulfilled is one in which freedom of enterprise is not regulated by justice, in which the private ownership of the means of production in the hands of very few families allows them to accumulate too much wealth, even when justly earned by their massive contribution to its production, so that many individuals and families are rendered destitute.

A just economy, whether achieved by *communism* (which is more accurately called state capitalism without freedom of enterprise) or by *socialized capitalism* (sometimes called the mixed economy because it retains private ownership of capital with some limitations upon it, and also freedom of enterprise with some government regulation of it), is one in which no one is destitute, in which all individuals or families participate in the general economic welfare, at least to the extent that all have the degree of wealth to which everyone is entitled on the basis of needs, and in which some have more wealth justly earned by the greater contribution they make to its production.

That is why we apply the phrase "welfare state" to states that have adopted state capitalism as well as to states that have adopted socialized capitalism. Both alike try to fulfill the precepts of socialism, though only the first try to do so by measures associated with communism rather than with private property and free enterprise.

In presenting the precepts of socialism as maxims of justice in the economic sphere, establishing an equality of economic conditions at the base line, accompanied by an inequality in degree above the base line, I have so far omitted one other maxim of great importance. It is the maxim that both Marx and Khrushchev put first: "From each according to his ability." That precept precedes "To each according to his needs" and "To each according to his contribution."

This maxim calls for two comments. First, it must be pointed out that, in any population, some are not able to make any contribution to the production of wealth. This runs parallel to the fact that, in the political sphere, some are not able to participate by exercising political power—infants and the pathologically disabled. They must be taken care of by families, by private charities, or as wards of the state. Their disfranchisement is just.

In the economic sphere, infants must also be taken care of, either by families or as wards of the state. In addition, there are individuals who suffer disabilities that render them unable to make any contribution to the production of wealth. They, too, must be taken care of, either by families, by private charities, or by the state.

Their basic economic needs are the same as those of their more fortunate fellows who are able to contribute to production and do so according to their abilities. Justice requires that their economic needs be satisfied by having enough wealth to live decent human lives, even if they cannot rise above the base line by earning more than that through the contribution they make.

This leaves us with a third group—those who have the ability requisite to engage in the production of wealth but cannot find employment in the economic sphere and, therefore, cannot earn by work either the minimal sufficiency that everyone needs or more than that. Justice requires that they be sustained by welfare payments, but *only* if their inability to find work is no fault of their own.

The welfare payments received by those who are both able and willing to earn a living, but cannot do so because they are unemployed through no fault of their own, make them dependents in the way that children are. This is an indignity that no adult human being should be forced to suffer. To avoid the injustice thus suffered by individuals able and willing to work, economic arrangements are thoroughly just only when they make it possible for everyone who is able to earn a living by contributing to the production of wealth to do so either to a degree that earns the decent livelihood that is enough to satisfy economic needs or to a degree that earns more wealth than that, within the limitation specified earlier.

The second comment to be made on the maxim "From each according to his ability" concerns the degrees of ability that underlie the different degrees of contribution that individuals can make.

These differences come, first of all, from differences in native endowment. Some are born with talents or aptitudes that make them able to make a greater contribution than that which can be made by others with inferior endowments.

Another explanation of different degrees of ability looks to what use individuals make of their inborn talents and aptitudes —the degree to which, by their own efforts, they fulfill their innate capacities. Those who start equal in the degree of their endowments may end up unequal in the degree of their attainments. It is even possible for individuals with inferior endowments to attain a development of themselves that surpasses attainments achieved by individuals of superior endowments. The former do so by making more of their inborn gifts than the latter.

Still another explanation lies in the favorable or unfavorable circumstances under which individuals make the effort to develop themselves. Those deprived of adequate schooling, for example, may thereby be prevented from making good use of their inborn gifts. As a result, their ultimate attainments may be inferior to those achieved by others who, with inferior endowments, have the advantage of better schooling.

Schooling is only one instance of many circumstantial factors that can influence the degree of ability an individual attains. Favorable circumstances facilitate reaching greater attainments; unfavorable circumstances hinder individuals from achieving all they can.

Considerations of justice, therefore, recommend that "From each according to his ability" together with "To each according to his contribution" works out equitably only when the circumstances (under which unequally endowed individuals make equal efforts to reach attainments that fully realize their innate capacities) are equally favorable to the success of such efforts.

The point just made introduces equality of opportunity into the picture. For inequality in attainments to result justly from inequality of endowments, given equal effort on the part of the unequally endowed, individuals must have an equal opportunity to exercise their talents and aptitudes, and put them to good use.

For inequality in attainments justly achieved to result in an unequal earning of wealth according to the precepts of justice we have been considering, all must have an equal opportunity to employ their innate and acquired abilities in productive work.

In addition, equal opportunity for employment should operate in a manner that engages those of superior ability, whether innate or acquired, in tasks or functions that are more productive. When those of superior ability are forced by unfavorable circumstances to take inferior jobs, equality of opportunity is not working as it should.

Equality of opportunity does not come into conflict with equality of condition when the latter is given precedence, as it should be because it is based on the first principle of justice: To all equally according to their needs.

Nor does it come into conflict with the inequalities of condition that justice also requires when these result from the operation of the second principle of justice: To each in varying degrees according to the functions performed or to the contributions made.

On the contrary, equality of opportunity facilitates the just operation of that second principle by providing equally favorable circumstances for all to make the most of their unequal talents and aptitudes and to put their acquired virtues, moral and intellectual, to the best use in political activity and in the production of wealth.

CHAPTER 24

The Domain of Justice

AT THE OPENING OF PART FOUR, in Chapter 18, I pointed out that these three ideas—liberty, equality, and justice—are closely related to one another and that justice permeates the discussion of the other two. We have now seen that that is the case, especially in certain parallelisms that appeared in the treatment of liberty and equality. Also, in our consideration of liberty and equality, we learned a great deal about justice—what it allows and what it requires. Now let us consider justice in itself without reference to liberty and equality.

The domain of justice is divided into two main spheres of interest. One is concerned with the justice of the individual in relation to other human beings and to the organized community itself—the state. The other is concerned with the justice of the state—its form of government and its laws, its political institutions and economic arrangements—in relation to the human beings that constitute its population.

Two serious errors that affect our understanding of justice have already been touched on and corrected in earlier chapters of this book, explicitly or by implication.

One, the mistake of giving primacy or precedence to the right over the good, had its origin in the moral philosophy of Immanuel Kant and was given currency in this century in a book, *The Right and the Good*, published by an Oxford philosopher, Professor W. D. Ross, in the early thirties. It stems from ignorance of the distinction between real and apparent goods—goods needed and goods wanted—an ignorance that could have been repaired by a more perceptive reading of Aristotle's *Ethics*.

Once that distinction is acknowledged and its full significance understood, it will be seen at once that it is impossible to know what is right and wrong in the conduct of one individual toward another until and unless one knows what is really good for each of them and for everyone else as well.

Real goods, based on natural needs, are convertible into natural rights, based on those same needs. To wrong another person is to violate his natural right to some real good, thereby depriving him of its possession and consequently impeding or interfering with his pursuit of happiness. To wrong or injure him in this way is the paradigm of one individual's injustice to another.

In short, one cannot do good and avoid injuring or doing evil to others without knowing what is really good for them. The only goods anyone has a natural right to are real, not apparent, goods. We do not have a natural right to the things we want; only to those we need.

"To each according to his wants," far from being a maxim of justice, makes no practical sense at all; for, if put into practice, it would result in what Thomas Hobbes called "the war of each against all," a state of affairs he also described as "nasty, brutish, and short."

If, as Professor Ross maintained, the right had primacy over the good, we should be able to determine what is right or just in our conduct toward others without any consideration of what is really good for them. But that is impossible.

The second mistake, equally serious for the subject at hand, made its appearance more recently in a widely discussed and overpraised book, *A Theory of Justice*, written by Harvard professor John Rawls. The error consists in identifying justice with fairness in the dealings of individuals with one another as well as in actions taken by society in dealing with its members.

Fairness, as we have seen, consists in treating equals equally and unequals unequally in proportion to their inequality. That is only one of several principles of justice, by no means the only principle and certainly not the primary one.

If, as Professor Rawls maintained, justice consists solely in fairness, murdering someone, committing mayhem, breaching a promise, falsely imprisoning another, enslaving him, libeling him, maliciously deceiving him, and rendering him destitute, would not be unjust, for there is no unfairness in any of these acts. They are all violations of rights, not violations of the precept that equals should be treated equally.

Only when the facts of human equality and inequality in personal respects and in the functions or services that persons perform provide the basis for determining what is just and unjust can justice and injustice be identified with fairness and unfairness.

When, on the contrary, the determination of what is just and unjust rests on the needs and rights inherent in human nature, then justice and injustice are based on what is really good and evil for human beings, not upon their personal equality or inequality or upon the equality and inequality of their performances.

The fact that all human beings, by nature equal, are also equally endowed with natural rights does not make their equality or their equal possession of rights the basis of a just treatment of them. If only two human beings existed, one could be unjust to the other by maliciously deceiving or falsely imprisoning him. That wrongful act can be seen as unjust without any reference to equality or inequality. It is unjust because it violates a right.

Murder, mayhem, rape, abduction, libel, breach of promise, false imprisonment, enslavement, subjection to despotic power, perjury, theft—these and many other violations of the moral or civil law are all unjust without being in any way unfair. They are all violations of natural or legal rights. That is what their injustice consists in, not unfairness.

Murder wrongfully deprives an individual of his right to life. Mayhem, torture, assault and battery wrongfully impair the health of an individual, which is a real good to which he has a natural right. False imprisonment, enslavement, subjection to despotic power transgress the individual's right to liberty. Libel, perjury, theft take away from individuals what is rightfully theirs—their good name, the truth they have a right to, property that is theirs by natural or legal right. Rendering others destitute, leaving them without enough wealth to lead decent human lives, deprives them of the economic goods to which they have a natural right.

In all these instances of injustice, which consist in the violation of rights, the ultimate injury done the unjustly treated individual lies in the effect it has upon his or her pursuit of happiness. The circumstances under which individuals live and the treatment they receive from other individuals or from the state are just to the extent that they facilitate his pursuit of happiness, unjust to the extent that they impair, impede, or frustrate that pursuit.

Unfairness enters the picture when unjustifiable discrimination takes place. To pay women less than men when they hold the same job and perform the same function equally well is an unjust discrimination. It is unjust because it is unfair. It treats equals unequally.

Difference in gender is a totally irrelevant consideration, as is difference in skin color, difference in ethnic origin, difference in religion. These differences being irrelevant, the persons involved are equal. They are, therefore, equally entitled to be considered for a job if one is open. And, when hired, they are entitled to equal compensation if they perform equally well. To treat them unequally is to discriminate among them unjustly, and that is unfair.

It is also unfair and therefore unjust not to discriminate when discrimination is required because relevant considerations are present. Not to give greater rewards to those who do more is unfair. Children of a tender age are quickly sensitive to such unfairness. When parents, who have assigned siblings certain household chores, reward equally the child who has discharged his assigned duties and the child who either has not done so or has done much less, the child who is aggrieved by the manifest injustice of his parents will cry out, "That's unfair."

Unfairness occurs in any transaction between individuals when, in an exchange of goods or services, one receives less than he deserves and one gets more than he deserves. The butcher who defrauds his customer by weighting his scales exacts an unfair price for the meat the customer is buying. The employer who pays an employee less than the going rate for the work to be done, because the latter is in such dire need that he will take the job at any wage, commits an injustice that is unfairness. He is giving the employee less money than he deserves. Fair wages and fair prices are prime examples of justice in exchange.

Unfairness occurs in distributions as well as in exchanges. When two soldiers who have performed heroic actions far beyond the call of duty both receive the Congressional Medal of Honor, the awards have been fairly allotted; but when one who has done as much as the other, by applicable standards of bravery, receives a less honorable citation than the other, the distribution of honors is manifestly unfair and unjust.

This is particularly true if the unfairly treated individual has been unjustly discriminated against because of irrelevant considerations, such as gender, race, or religion. Such unfairness, stemming from unjust discrimination, occurs in appointments to public office when candidates of equal merit are not given equal consideration because of differences among them that have nothing to do with their ability to discharge the duties of the office. The nondiscriminatory character of justice is symbolically epitomized by the blindfold on the eyes of the statue.

It may be thought that the use of the word "deserves" in our discussion of fairness—a woman getting less pay than she deserves, a soldier awarded an inferior honor getting less than he deserves, a customer defrauded by his butcher giving less than he deserves—introduces the notion of rights into our understanding of fairness. It certainly can be said that what a person deserves he or she has a right to. If that which an individual has a right to is something he or she deserves, why is not every injustice that is a violation of rights also an instance of unfairness?

The answer derives from which consideration comes first in the determination of what is just or unjust.

When what the individual deserves is based on what he has a natural or legal right to, that right is the criterion for regarding an action as unjust because it is violated.

When what an individual deserves is determined by comparison with what another individual also deserves, and when the comparison is made with respect to what both individuals have done or are able to do, then the equality or inequality of their performance or of their ability to perform is the criterion for regarding the treatment accorded them as just or unjust because it is fair or unfair.

Fairness and unfairness in distributions to individuals always involve some comparison of the merits or deserts of the individuals concerned, and that comparison always involves considerations of equality and inequality. Fairness and unfairness in exchanges between individuals always involve some comparison of the value of the things being exchanged, and that comparison also always involves considerations of equality and inequality. Therein lies the essence of the justice and injustice that is identified with fairness and unfairness.

In contrast, the injustice that is identified with a violation of rights calls for no comparison of the merit of one individual with that of another, or comparison of the value of one thing with another. Nor does it involve considerations of equality and inequality. The existence of a right in just one individual suffices to make any action that transgresses that right an unjust act.

It would appear that the definition of justice at the beginning of Justinian's codification of Roman law—"the constant and perpetual will to render to each what is his due"—covers both justice as securing rights from violation and also justice as fair treatment. However, what appears to be the case is only superficially true. Justinian's definition covers both forms of justice while neglecting to observe their difference.

What is due an individual or what an individual deserves can be determined either (1) by the criterion of what he deserves by right, either his natural rights or rights granted him by the law of the state; or (2) by the comparison of one individual with another according to their merits, either in terms of what they can do or in terms of what they have done.

These two forms of desert are irreducible to one another, as are the injustice that consists in the violation of rights and the injustice that consists in unfair distributions or exchanges. There is still a third form of injustice that is irreducible to the other two.

The natural moral law puts us under three obligations. Its first precept commands us to seek the good and avoid evil, which, spelled out, means seek everything that is really good for us and so is an indispensable ingredient in making one's whole life good.

This first precept is not a principle of justice because it concerns the individual's conduct of his private life. Only the second and third precepts of the natural law are principles of justice. They concern the conduct of an individual in relation to others.

The second precept of the natural moral law commands us to do good and avoid doing evil, which, spelled out, means acting justly toward others, either (*a*) by not violating their rights and thus not impeding or frustrating their pursuit of happiness, or (*b*) by treating them fairly rather than unfairly in distributions and exchanges.

The third precept commands us to act for the common good or general welfare of the community of which we are members. This is the contributive aspect of justice. It cannot be reduced to the two forms of justice identified above as subordinate aspects of the second precept of the natural moral law, any more than either of those two forms can be reduced to one another.

For example, the citizen who commits treason does something inimical to the security and welfare of the state. He has not injured other citizens directly by violating their rights or by treating them unfairly in relation to one another. Similarly, the citizen who bribes a public official to achieve an illicit result corrupts due process of law and thereby acts contrary to the general interest of the community that prospers under the rule of law.

The public official who acts unconstitutionally by exceeding the authority vested in his office by the constitution commits a grave injustice, one that directly injures the community as a whole and only indirectly its members. It may even be said that the ordinary citizen who fails to exercise his suffrage is defective with respect to contributive justice and that that defect adversely affects the political process and so is contrary to the general welfare.

The ordering of the three precepts of the natural moral law confirms what has already been said about the primacy of the good over the right.

The pursuit of happiness is our primary obligation. Doing what is right with regard to others and doing what is right with regard to the community as a whole are secondary and tertiary obligations.

Their subordination to the first precept and to our primary

obligation lies in the fact that our doing what is right, either with regard to other individuals or to the community as a whole, affects everyone's pursuit of happiness, which is the ultimate and common good of all.

It affects it directly, but in a negative way, by not impeding or frustrating anyone's efforts to make a good life for himself or herself. It affects it indirectly, in a positive way, by contributing to the welfare of the community as a whole, which in turn redounds to the benefit of its individual members in their pursuit of happiness.

The distinction just noted between the direct and indirect effects of just acts on the part of individuals leads us to another insight concerning justice. The individual is under no positive obligation of justice to act in such a fashion that others directly benefit from his action. Justice does not consist in doing good directly to others. Justice consists only in giving what is due, what is deserved.

In contrast, the benevolent impulses of love go beyond justice to benefit the loved individual without regard to strict deserts. The generosity of love is gratuitous in its gifts. In contrast, the awards of justice are heartlessly exact. That is why they must sometimes be softened by mercy and dispensed with equity that expresses the spirit rather than the letter of the law.

Justice restricts itself to what others deserve, either because they have a right to it or because they deserve to be treated fairly. This requires actions that benefit them negatively, not positively—by *not* violating their rights, by *not* treating them unfairly.

Individuals act positively for the benefit of others when they discharge the obligation of justice to contribute to the general welfare. In this way they do benefit others, but only indirectly through the participation of all in the welfare of the community, especially its peace and its prosperity.

We come, finally, to the justice of the organized community itself in relation to the good of its individual members. Here we are chiefly concerned with the justice of its form of government, the justice of its economic arrangements, and the justice of its positive, or man-made, laws.

In the sphere of political institutions, the most just form of government is a republic with universal suffrage and with a constitution that includes a bill of economic as well as political rights that secures the natural rights of all. The supreme justice of a constitutional democracy resides in its distribution of political liberty and political equality to all, with the exception of infants and the pathologically disabled, as well as in the protection of other natural rights.

In the sphere of economic arrangements, the most just economy is the one that provides all individuals and families with equal participation in the general economic welfare at least to the extent that all have, on the base line, the degree of wealth needed for a decent human life. No one is left destitute by being deprived of that minimal sufficiency. Above the base line, additional justice is done by a distribution of wealth that is fair because it gives some haves more and some haves less in proportion to the contribution they make to the production of wealth.

If socialism be the right name for measures that promote economic justice, then the most just society is a socialist, democratic republic.

The justice meted out by the man-made laws of the state derives, first of all, from the enactment in positive laws of specific determinations of those principles of the natural moral law that are its precepts of natural justice. The rules of positive law are just to the extent that they prevent natural rights from being violated and to the extent that they preserve or promote fairness in exchanges and in distributions.

Rules of positive law may also consist in determinations of that precept of natural justice which calls for actions that preserve or promote the general welfare. Laws regulating public assemblies with a view to maintaining peace and order are of this sort; so, too, are tax laws that provide revenue for public services as well as for the support of government itself. These may, in addition, be just or unjust in the manner in which they fairly or unfairly distribute the burdens of taxation.

Last, we come to rules of positive law that do not derive in any way from precepts of natural justice. They command or prohibit what is otherwise morally indifferent—neither just nor unjust in itself. They legislate about matters that must be regulated for the public interest, either in one way or another, neither way being inherently right or wrong.

Traffic regulations are a prime example of laws the only justice of which consists in the fact that, once they are made, compliance with them serves the good of the community. Infractions have the opposite result. Hence the individual who obeys or disobeys such regulations is contributively just or unjust.

CHAPTER 25

The Justice and the Authority
of Law

THE MAN-MADE LAW OF THE STATE derives its authority from justice in each of three ways: (1) by the enactment of measures that protect natural rights; (2) by legislation that prescribes or safeguards fairness in transactions among individuals; (3) by regulating matters affected with the public interest for the general welfare of the community.

Not anyone at all can make a law that has authority. Authoritative legislation resides with those who have been constitutionally authorized to legislate for the welfare of the community. That is the authority vested in a legislative body set up by the constitution.

In states under despotic governments, the power to make laws is in the hands of a king or prince, but the absolute sovereign imposes rules sheerly by might, not by right. In the mixed regimes that existed in the Middle Ages, regimes that were partly absolute and partly constitutional, the authoritative source of law was the immemorial customs of the realm. The king had authority to govern, to enforce the law, and to decide by edict matters outside the reach of law, but not to legislate. The legitimacy of the throne's occupant was often challenged by contenders to the throne.

In addition to having the authority that positive law derives from its being made by persons authorized to legislate and from its being just in accordance with the precepts of natural justice, it also wields the strong arm of coercive force to command compliance from those who do not recognize its authority. The authority of the positive law lies in its expression of what is right and wrong for individuals to do. Its coercive force lies in the might or power of the state to make the rule of law effective.

Naked right—right without might, authority devoid of power—may speak with the tongue of angels, but it will not serve for the government of a community of men and women. "If men were angels," Alexander Hamilton wrote, "no government would be necessary"—that is, no government exercising coercive force to make its authority effective. The contrary view is the dream of utopian anarchists who imagine a blissful community in which human beings live together in peace and concord without any application of coercive force.

Naked might—might without right, power devoid of authority—is no utopian dream. It is a harsh reality that has existed from the beginning of recorded time.

Absolute despotisms of every variety, tyrannical and benevolent, antedated constitutional governments in antiquity. They came into existence again with the overthrow of ancient republics, as in the Greece of Alexander and the Rome of the Caesars. They emerged once again with the dissolution of the mixed regimes at the end of the Middle Ages. They exist in the world today in forms more oppressive than the tyrannies of antiquity.

That would be bad enough if living under a just government and just laws, with its attendant benefits of liberty and equality, were not, along with peace, one of the greatest of the circumstantial goods that can bless human life and aid or abet the pursuit of happiness.

What is worse is that despotism is defended by political philosophers, by philosophers of law, by jurists and lawyers. They often do so, it must be conceded, without realizing that the position they take with regard to the relation of law and justice leads to this dire consequence. Still, it is difficult to understand how they can be so blind to the conclusions that inexorably flow from what appears to be the basic error they make in the beginning—not only basic, but also egregious.

That basic error consists in giving law precedence and primacy over justice, rather than the other way around. Instead of regarding natural justice as the fountainhead from which man-made law springs, the source of its authority and the measure of its legitimacy, the view here being criticized turns things upside down. It regards positive law, the man-made law of the state, as the sole source of justice, the only determination of what it is right and wrong for individuals to do in relation to one another and to the community itself.

These conflicting views concerning the relation of law and justice have come to be called the naturalist and the positivist views of the matter.

The naturalists, as that name indicates, affirm the existence of natural justice, of natural and unalienable rights, of the natural moral law, and of valid prescriptive oughts that elicit our assent, both independently of and prior to the existence of positive law.

The positivists deny all this and affirm the opposite. For them, the positive law—the man-made law of the state—provides the only prescriptive oughts that human beings are compelled to obey. According to them, nothing is just or unjust until it has been declared so by a command or prohibition of positive law.

If this is a fundamentally erroneous view, as I think it is, its ultimate roots lie very deep. They rise from the most profound mistake that can be made in our thinking about good and evil. It is the mistake made by those who embrace an unattenuated subjectivism and relativism with respect to what is good and bad, right and wrong.

Neglecting or rejecting the distinction between real and apparent goods, together with that between natural needs and acquired wants, the positivists can find no basis for the distinction between what *ought* to be desired or done and what *is* desired or done. From that flows the further consequence that there is no natural moral law, no natural rights, no natural justice, ending up with the conclusion that man-made law alone determines what is just and unjust, right and wrong.

This positivist view is as ancient as the despotisms that existed in antiquity. It was first eloquently expressed in the opening book of Plato's *Republic* where Thrasymachus, responding to Socrates' mention of the view that justice consists in rendering what is due, declared and defended the opposite view— that justice is the interest of the stronger. Spelled out, this means that what is just or unjust is determined solely by whoever has the power to lay down the law of the land.

The positivist view is recurrent in later centuries with the recurrence of later despotisms. It was expressed by the Roman jurisconsult, Ulpian, who, defending the absolutism of the Caesars, declared that whatever pleases the prince has the force of law. Still later, in the sixteenth century, the same view was set forth by another defender of absolute government, Thomas Hobbes, in *The Leviathan;* and later, in the nineteenth century, by John Austin, in his *Analytical Jurisprudence.*

Neither Austin nor the twentieth-century legal positivists who follow him regard themselves as defenders of absolute government or despotism. That is what they are, however— perhaps not as explicitly as their predecessors, but by implication at least.

The denial of natural rights, the natural moral law, and natural justice leads not only to the positivist conclusion that man-made law alone determines what is just and unjust. It also leads to a corollary which inexorably attaches itself to that conclusion —that might makes right. This is the very essence of absolute or despotic government.

According to the naturalist view, espoused by Plato, Aristotle, Augustine, Thomas Aquinas, John Locke, and J. J. Rousseau, an unjust positive law is a law in name only. Lacking the authority that can be derived only from constitutionally authorized legislation and from determinations made with respect to antecedent principles of natural justice, it has coercive force and that alone. Force without authority is might without right.

When what is just or unjust is thought to be determined solely by whoever has the power to lay down the law of the land, it unavoidably follows that the law of the land cannot be judged either just or unjust.

The law of the state being the sole measure of justice, there is no way to measure the justice and injustice of positive laws. It is even redundant—or worse, self-contradictory—to speak of just positive laws. They are neither just nor unjust; they simply are. What they prescribe becomes the just thing to do; what they prohibit becomes unjust.

What has just been said about positive laws must also be said about states and governments, political institutions and economic arrangements. None of these can be called just; one cannot be compared with another as more or less just; all are beyond criticism as unjust; none can be subject to reform or rebellion on the ground that its grievous injustice must be rectified.

Obliterated are the right and duty to rebel against governments that violate unalienable rights, and to institute new governments that will secure these rights and derive their just powers from the consent of the governed. Legal positivism rejects the Declaration of Independence, not only its initial premises, but also the revolutionary conclusions to which they lead. Revolutionary rhetoric, yes; but revolutionary reasons, no.

In Greek antiquity, the Sophists, who were the first law professors and also the first positivists, appealed to the difference between nature and Convention. Fire burns alike in Greece and in Persia, they said, but the laws of Greece differ from laws of Persia because they are wholly matters of convention, with no natural basis. Hence what is just and unjust, or right and wrong, is one thing in Greece, and quite another in Persia.

When justice is thus made entirely a matter of convention and completely subsidiary to the enactments of positive law, what is just and unjust necessarily varies from place to place and from time to time. To take two prime examples, chattel slavery and the political disfranchisement of women are just in one country and not in another, and, in a particular country, they are just at one time and not at another, according to the legal enactments enforced at one or another place and time. So, too, with regard to laws that discriminate among human beings with regard to race and religion as well as gender. The discriminations were once just when they were on the lawbooks and enforced. They become unjust later, when those laws are repealed and no longer enforced.

There are still further consequences of the positivist view of law and justice. These can be seen by remembering what was said earlier about there being no loss of liberty in human actions that are regulated by just laws. It is also necessary to remember that what was said earlier reflected views quite contrary to the underlying premises of positivism.

When a virtuous person obeys a just law, he does so voluntarily. He freely chooses to act in compliance with the law because what the law commands him to do he would willingly do anyway, since what a just law commands he himself recognizes to be the right thing to do. He responds to the authority that the law has for him because of its justice. He is under no compulsion to obey the law because of its coercive force and the threat of punishment.

The bad man, who, from lack of a virtuous will, refrains from criminal acts *only* because of the law's coercive force and his fear of being caught and punished, does not act freely when he obeys the law. He does so under compulsion, and only as a matter of expediency. He responds only to the force of the law, not to its authority.

Were he to overcome his fear, and think it expedient to disobey the law, his disobedience would not be an expression of liberty on his part, but an indulgence in license. In either case, his compliance with or infraction of the law stems from what he judges to be expedient or inexpedient, not what he acknowledges to be just or unjust.

The positivist view of law and justice puts us all in the position of the bad man. If laws are neither just nor unjust, nothing but their coercive force compels us to obey them. Our decision to obey or disobey them must rest solely on considerations of expediency. We can disobey them with no pang of conscience and we can do so with impunity if we are clever enough to do so without getting caught and punished.

In one respect and only one, there is some truth in the positivist view. As pointed out earlier, some laws, such as traffic ordinances, command or prohibit actions that are otherwise morally indifferent. In themselves, they are neither just nor unjust. What they command or prohibit becomes just or unjust only after the laws are made in the public interest and for the general welfare. Even then, the very opposite of the regulation adopted would often serve the general welfare as well.

Driving on the wrong side of the road and parking in the wrong place are instances of what the criminal law calls *mala prohibita*—things that are wrong only because they are prohibited by the ordinances of the community.

In contradistinction, committing mayhem, stealing, and kidnapping are instances of *mala per se*—things that should be regarded as wrong even if no positive law prohibited them. They are wrong because they are violations of natural rights and natural justice even though the state does not secure these rights by its ordinances, nor does it enact positive laws that make determinations of natural justice in these respects.

The positivist view must perforce reject the distinction between *mala prohibita* and *mala per se*. All wrongful actions are simply *mala prohibita*—wrongful because they are prohibited by law.

According to the naturalist view of *mala prohibita*, even the ordinances that make certain acts just or unjust have an element of justice in them, but one that is not based on either natural rights or fairness.

According to the third precept of the natural moral law, we as individuals are under an obligation to act for the common good of the community. It sometimes becomes highly expedient for those given the authority and responsibility to legislate to lay down ordinances that command individuals to act as they should for the common good. Laws made for this purpose are, therefore, both just and expedient, and just because expedient.

Western thinking about justice began with the Greeks. At its very beginning, in Plato's dialogues, we are confronted with the fundamental issues about law and justice and about justice and expediency. The dispute between Socrates and Thrasymachus, the sophist, introduces us to the conflict between the naturalist and the positivist views of law and justice. Even more extraordinary is Plato's probing, in the *Republic* and again in the *Gorgias*, of questions about justice and expediency. He stands out as the one Western philosopher who is most insistent about asking the two most difficult questions concerning justice.

The first of these questions asks us to consider why we should be just. Only because it is expedient to do so? Or because being just toward others, whether or not commanded by the law of the state, is an indispensable factor in our achieving happiness for ourselves?

The other question presents us with alternative options—to do injustice to others or suffer injustice at their hands. Which option should we choose if we must take one or the other? And why?

Justice is not the only one of these six great ideas about which such important issues have been raised and such important questions asked. No idea is a great idea unless it raises important issues and is the focal point of important questions. I will attempt to explore such issues and questions, with respect to truth, goodness, and beauty, as well as liberty, equality, and justice, in the fourth and concluding part of this book.

PART FOUR
Epilogue: Great Issues and Questions

CHAPTER 26

Ideas, Issues, Questions

IN THE COURSE OF THE PRECEDING CHAPTERS, I have not hesitated to take a definite position on or advance a definite view concerning the ideas under consideration.

The great ideas being the main subjects of controversy in the tradition of Western thought, readers must realize that the account given of the six ideas treated in this book represents a point of view about them—well considered, representing many years of reflection, yet nevertheless one point of view about matters concerning which others disagree with the opinions expressed.

In some instances, I have called the reader's attention to views that I think are untenable, and I have tried to persuade the reader to accept my judgment.

In some instances, I have presented conflicting views. There

I have tried to show how the conflict can be resolved, especially when the opposite sides on a particular issue represent half-truths that can be reconciled.

In still other instances, I have indicated questions that remain to be answered without doing more than intimating what the range of answers might be.

I have not gone far enough in the direction of exposing all the fundamental issues, all the disputed questions, and some of the unanswered ones, which constitute the controversies that have centered around each of these six ideas in the course of twenty-five centuries of Western thought. Nor can I undertake to overcome that failure. That undertaking would call for an effort too comprehensive to be accomplished in a small book.

The Institute for Philosophical Research has made that comprehensive effort only once—in dealing with the idea of freedom. The two volumes published on that subject in 1958 and 1961 were the product of more than six years of reading and discussion, engaging the minds of more than twenty-five people working cooperatively. The two volumes, comprising about fifteen hundred pages, were heavily burdened with footnotes. They were laced with quotations from the authors whose opinions were reviewed and compared. They carried bibliographies citing works studied and works examined running in number well over five hundred. They examined a half dozen major controversies, each involving numerous issues. The exploration of the controversy about the freedom of the will and free choice, broken down into four main issues, occupied more than three hundred pages.

I mention all this to explain why the brief enumeration I am going to make, in the next two chapters, of important issues and questions concerning truth, goodness, and beauty, and of liberty, equality, and justice, must necessarily be inadequate. Nevertheless, it may serve to give readers some slight realization of what remains to be done by anyone who wishes to push his own thinking further on any of these subjects.

To achieve a decent brevity, for which I am sure readers will be grateful, I shall have to be highly selective. My criterion of selection will be to choose issues and questions that have a direct and significant bearing on matters treated in the preceding chapters of this book. In a few instances, I may attempt to indicate how a basic conflict among competing theories can be resolved, or how an important question might be answered.

Readers who have already begun to challenge or query the views I have expressed in the preceding chapters, as well as readers who may be stimulated to do so by what is set forth in the two remaining chapters, can go much further. The exploration of the intellectual intricacies of any great idea is an almost endless process. It is also a most rewarding adventure, the most pleasurable and profitable use of one's mind by anyone who enjoys thinking, which is the reason Plato called philosophizing "that dear delight."

CHAPTER 27

Concerning Truth, Goodness, and Beauty

THE DEFINITION OF TRUTH as consisting in the agreement of the mind with reality, or the correspondence between what we think and what is or is not in fact the way things are, rests on a number of assumptions that have been challenged.

One is the assumption that there is a realm of existence independent of the human mind and of what it thinks. Another is that this reality has a determinate character. Were it totally indeterminate, no statement about it could be either true or false, and diametrically opposite statements about it could both be true or both be false.

The principle of contradiction would not be a basic rule of thought, to be followed in our efforts to get at the truth. We could, at one and the same time, think that a certain state of affairs existed and also that it did not exist, and be none the worse for that in our thinking.

In denying that there is any truth or falsity, the extreme skeptic must ultimately either deny that an independent reality exists or deny that it has a determinate character with which our thinking either corresponds or fails to correspond. It should be obvious at once that, in going to this extreme, the skeptic necessarily contradicts himself. Unless he claims truth for his assertion that there is no independent reality or that it does not have a determinate character, his own position vanishes; and if he does claim truth for his denials, he must do so on grounds that ultimately presuppose the definition of truth.

Should the extreme skeptic not be deterred by the charge of self-contradiction, we have only two choices left in dealing with him. One is to discontinue the conversation as utterly fruitless. The other is to put his position to the pragmatic test.

The pragmatic theory of truth, eloquently stated and ably defended by the American philosopher William James at the beginning of this century, was often misconstrued to be a new definition of truth. On the contrary, it accepted the traditional so-called correspondence theory of truth and proceeded to offer useful indications or criteria for determining whether a given statement was true or false.

The pragmatic view that an opinion is true if it works and false if it fails to work does not tell us what truth is but rather whether the opinion in question is true or false. An individual in a boat drifting downstream is of the opinion that a dangerous cataract is four miles off, when in fact it is only one mile distant. If he relies on that opinion to take a short nap in the sunshine, he will end up in a disaster. The falsity of his opinion is clearly revealed by its not working as he expected.

An opinion passes the pragmatic test by working as we expect it to only if it corresponds with the way things are. It fails to work when it fails to correspond. Its working or not working is a test of its truth, not a definition of what its truth consists in. The extreme skeptic may think he can reject the correspondence theory of what truth is, but can he—does he—reject the pragmatic test as well?

Apologists for that most extreme of nihilistic philosophers, Friedrich Nietzsche, find themselves obliged to admit that he, while throwing truth out the front window, allowed it to come in through the back door by accepting, however grudgingly, the pragmatic test. Not to do so in the world of action is so obviously suicidal that it cannot fail to overcome the extreme dogmatism of the extreme skeptic.

The pragmatic test of the truth or falsity of particular opinions has significance for us beyond the yeoman service it performs in the refutation of skepticism. It raises a question about what is often called "prediction and verification" as a way of telling whether a particular opinion is true or false.

It has sometimes been supposed, and it is still popularly thought, that if a prediction is confirmed, that verifies the opinion upon which the prediction is based. When an opinion we hold leads us to expect a certain result and that result occurs, the opinion we have acted on has worked successfully. The opinion having passed the pragmatic test, we regard it as true.

There seems to be no valid objection to this view of the matter in the case of opinions about particular matters of fact; for example, that the cataract downstream is only one mile farther. But when we come to generalizations—to statements that are supposed to be true universally or without exception—prediction and verification does not have the same effect.

Any statement that either explicitly or implicitly claims to hold for *all* instances—all without exception—cannot be established as definitely true by a finite number of observed instances that tend to confirm the opinion in question. The successive confirmations do not verify the generalization in the sense of showing it to be true with finality and certitude. They verify it only in the sense of showing it to be more and more probable; that is, increasing the degree of our assurance that the generalization is true.

Prediction and verification, or the application of the pragmatic test, goes beyond probability only when a negative instance falsifies a generalization. Since the generalization claims to hold universally, or without exception, a single exception, provided by one negative instance, falsifies it with certitude. Its falsity is final and incorrigible.

The notion of probability leads us to what, in my judgment, is the most difficult problem or issue in the sphere of our thinking about the idea of truth. The question can be put simply: Is all probability subjective, or, in certain areas of reality, does objective probability exist? Let me explain the question.

Objective probability signifies indeterminacy built into the structure of reality itself. Subjective probability measures degrees of uncertainty or doubt concerning the truth of our judgments about reality.

To say that all probability is subjective is to say that degrees of probability are always and only measures of the assurance with which we claim that a certain opinion is true or false. The opinion itself, in relation to reality, is either true or false; but when we do not know it to be true with certainty, as is usually the case, we affirm its truth with some degree of assurance less than certitude. When we then say that it is more or less probable, we are not saying that it is probable rather than true. We are saying that it is probably true, and that the degree of probability—the degree of our assurance about its truth—is more than zero and less than one.

The view that all probability is subjective, in the sense indicated above, presupposes that reality is completely determinate —that everything is either one way or another, but not both at the same time. The principle of contradiction is not only a law of thought, to be observed in our efforts to get at the truth. It is also a law of existence. Nothing can both exist and not exist at one and the same time; nor can anything both have and not have a certain characteristic at one and the same time. If the realm of real existence did not conform without exception to the principle of contradiction, that principle would not operate as a sound rule to observe in our efforts to get at the truth.

Games of chance confirm rather than challenge the view that probability is subjective rather than objective. Considering the next toss of a coin, we are compelled by the laws of chance to say that it is equally probable that it will fall heads up and that it will fall tails up. This means only that our degree of assurance in betting on heads is equal to our degree of assurance, or lack of it, in betting on tails. Though the two statements, "It will be heads," and, "It will be tails," are subjectively of equal probability, one of these two statements is objectively true and the other objectively false. We do not know which it will be, or rather we know only that there is a fifty-fifty chance of its being one or the other, but we do know with certitude that it will be one and not the other.

Future contingencies, such as whether it will snow on Christmas Day next year, are not indeterminate. The prediction that it will snow is either true or false right now, in advance of the event, but our prediction of what will happen when the time comes around falls far short of certitude. The probability we assign to that prediction's being true expresses our degree of assurance about it.

Nor do the statistical laws of nature run counter to the view that reality is completely determinate. They merely represent the kind of knowledge we have about certain phenomena, in contrast to the kind of knowledge that is expressed in causal laws. When a causal law is affirmed as true, in the light of all evidence available at the time, the prediction that a certain effect will result from the operation of certain antecedent conditions can be made at that time with certitude. A statistical law of nature enables us to predict certain physical states or events only with a degree of probability, not with certitude. But in both cases the physical phenomena themselves are equally determinate.

Until this century, the natural sciences did not challenge the view that reality is completely determinate and that probability is entirely subjective. The advent of quantum mechanics, in the sphere of subatomic physics, introduced what is generally known as the Heisenberg principle of indeterminacy, or, as it is sometimes called, the principle of uncertainty.

Experimentation that seeks to determine both the position and velocity of elementary, or subatomic, particles cannot fully succeed in both efforts. A certain quantum of indeterminacy, specified as h, cannot be eliminated with respect to either the position or velocity of the particle.

A highly exacerbated controversy ensued between Albert Einstein, on the one hand, and Niels Bohr and Werner Heisenberg, on the other.

Einstein defended the view that the indeterminacy encountered in quantum mechanics should be interpreted as a subjective probability. The probability that the electron occupies a definite position or moves with a definite velocity measures the degree of assurance with which we can assert that it is at that position or has that velocity. In reality, the electron either is at that position or not; it either has that velocity or not.

Bohr and Heisenberg, the leading exponents of the Copenhagen School, defended the opposite position and they have won most physicists over to their point of view. While reality may be, for the most part, determinate, it is indeterminate in the sphere of subatomic phenomena. The degree of uncertainty about the position or velocity of an electron is not just a measure of our ignorance, or lack of complete assurance about it. It points to an objective probability—an uncertainty or indeterminacy—in the way things in fact are.

To overcome the repugnance with which the mind reacts to such indeterminacy in reality, the Copenhagen School introduced what they called "the principle of complementarity." This, in effect, explained away the apparent violation of the principle of contradiction as a law governing reality as well as thought.

The indeterminacy of the position of an electron or a photon at a certain moment might appear to involve us in the contradiction of saying that it was both here and not here at the same time. But according to the principle of complementarity, its being both here and not here at a given moment can be explained by reference to different ways of viewing the same phenomenon, ways that are complementary rather than contradictory.

The difficult question we are left with is one that everyone must answer for himself. Does the principle of complementarity, which the Copenhagen School found it necessary to introduce in order to explain objective probability or real indeterminacy in the sphere of subatomic phenomena, implicitly involve the reaffirmation of the principle of contradiction as a law governing reality without exception? Does it reveal as well as conceal an admission that Einstein was right after all?

My own answer to these questions is affirmative, but I must admit that whenever I am in the company of scientists, I remain in a minority of one. In my view, the phenomena under consideration are not *in themselves indeterminate*. They have been rendered *indeterminable by us* as a result of the ways in which we are compelled to observe and measure them. The effect on them of our methods of observation makes the precision with which we can measure quantities in classical mechanics unattainable in the sphere of wave and quantum mechanics.

There is one other point of indeterminacy that should be mentioned. It occurs in the sphere of mathematics rather than physics. In 1931, Kurt Gödel published a paper on formally undecidable propositions in mathematics. It showed that a consistent, axiomatic mathematical system contains propositions that may be true, but the truth of which cannot be demonstrated in that system.

Of all the spheres of inquiry in which men are engaged in the pursuit of truth, mathematics is the one in which we have come to expect the most complete agreement among all who are competent to judge. Even in the light of Gödel's argument, that remains the case.

Disagreement among mathematicians about the truth of any formally decidable propositions would be scandalous. That, in any well-constructed mathematical system, there are formally undecidable propositions should not alter our expectations with regard to agreement among mathematicians.

Pivotal in our thinking about the idea of goodness is the distinction between real and apparent goods together with the distinction on which it is based—between specifically natural and individually acquired desires, or needs and wants. Without these two distinctions the line cannot be drawn that divides what is objectively good for all human beings and what is only subjectively good, differing from individual to individual and from time to time.

It should not be surprising that this pivotal point is also the focus of controversy in regard to goodness. The questions at issue are whether human needs can be clearly distinguished from individual wants, whether one man's needs are another man's wants, whether needs are unaffected by nurtural and other circumstantial conditions, and whether the satisfaction of needs calls for different goods or different amounts of the same good under different circumstances or for different individuals.

The view that certain things are really good for all human beings under all circumstances is inseparable from the view that there can be objectively true value judgments and prescriptions concerning what human beings ought to seek and ought to do. If the questions at issue about needs and wants cannot be satisfactorily answered, if the distinction between needs and wants is beclouded or blurred by inexpungeable doubts about its validity, the scales inevitably tilt in the direction of the subjectivist extreme, which holds that there is no objective truth in the sphere of value judgments. Whatever appears good to the individual according to his individual desires or predilections is good for him or her and may appear to be the very opposite to someone else. There is no basis for saying that anything ought or ought not to be desired.

As we have seen, the objectivity of truth presupposes the existence of an independent reality that is determinate in its structure and characteristics. The objectivity of goodness presupposes the existence of a human reality—a human nature that is determinate in its species-specific properties, among which are the inherent appetitive tendencies that constitute specially human needs. Individual members of the human species, being all equally human, are innately endowed with the same specifically human properties.

To affirm these truths about human nature and the human species is to affirm the universality of human needs, the same in all human individuals at all times and places and under all circumstances. These truths have been challenged in our century by social and behavioral scientists. At the extreme, it is held that nurtural and environmental circumstances are the primary, if not the exclusive, determinants of human characteristics.

What is called human nature is nothing but a plastic blob that can be shaped in a wide diversity of ways by differences in nurture and in social, economic, and political conditions. Marxists, for example, go to that extreme when they hold that a truly communist society will produce a "new man," radically different from the human beings who were nurtured and conditioned by the oppressive and competitive societies of the past.

I think that the constant and fixed character of human nature as something genetically determined in the case of the human species (as it is similarly determined in the case of other organic species) can be defended against the doubts or denials that have been leveled against it. But this by itself does not suffice to preserve the clarity of the distinction between human needs and individual wants. It is also necessary to answer the questions that have been raised about the effect of nurtural and other circumstantial factors upon the extent of human needs or what is required to satisfy them.

It must be conceded at once that nurtural and other circumstantial factors do affect the character of human needs and the things required for their satisfaction. Only one fact about human needs remains constant and fixed as a consequence of the constant and fixed character of human nature. The number of human needs has always been the same and will always be the same as long as the human species exists upon this planet.

Changes in the environment under which human beings are nurtured do not increase or decrease the number of their needs; nor, even with the number unchanged, does the naming of the needs enumerated change from time to time with alterations in the environmental circumstances.

What varies from time to time with alterations in the circumstances of human life are the instrumental or implemental factors required for the satisfaction of the invariant natural needs. A few examples may throw light on the point being made.

Man by nature desires to know; or, in other words, human beings, innately endowed with cognitive powers, have a natural tendency to seek knowledge. Knowledge is a real good that all human beings need. How is this need satisfied? In a wide variety of ways—sometimes by individual inquiry, sometimes by parental instruction, sometimes by the funded experience or beliefs of the tribe, sometimes by the institution of schools.

Do human beings need the formal education provided by a school system? Yes, but only as *one* way of implementing the satisfaction of their basic need for knowledge. The need for schooling is secondary or derivative, not primary or basic. Knowledge is always needed by human beings, but schooling is not.

Another example may be helpful. Health is a real good that all human beings need. But what is needed to implement the satisfaction of this need varies from time to time and place to place. Under the conditions of preindustrial economies, the basic need for health did not require implementation by the derivative need for air, water, and earth protected from pollution by noxious industrial wastes.

Do human beings have a natural need for means of transportation? No, but when, under the circumstances of urban as opposed to rural life, individuals must travel inconvenient distances to go to work to obtain the economic goods that are a basic human need, means of transportation may take on the character of an implemental need. Failure to understand the difference between a basic human need and what is needed to implement the satisfaction of that need leads to the erroneous conclusion that a new basic need has emerged with the emergence of urban, industrial life.

Means of transportation, environmental protection against pollution, the institution of school systems are all real goods, but only because wealth (or the means of subsistence), health, and knowledge are real goods, which, under certain circumstances, require them for their implementation. Wealth, health, and knowledge are always and everywhere real goods, no matter what the circumstances of human life may be. But means of transportation, environmental protection against pollution, and the institution of school systems are not, under all circumstances, required to implement the satisfaction of the basic human needs for the real goods just mentioned.

All human beings need sustenance and shelter. But the amount and character of the food and drink they need or of the kind of protection they need from the ravages of the environment will vary with the clement or inclement character of the climate in which they live and with the propitious or unpropitious character of the environmental circumstances that affect their lives. The need for food, drink, and shelter is invariant. What varies with variations in environmental circumstances is the quality or character of the things that satisfy these invariant needs.

The affirmation of natural needs underlies the affirmation of natural rights. All human beings have the same set of natural rights because all human beings have inherent needs for the same set of real goods. Every human being has a natural right to what any human being needs because it is really good for him to have.

Do all human beings have a natural right to means of transportation, to environmental protection against pollution, to formal schooling? No, because under certain circumstances these goods are not needed to implement the satisfaction of basic human needs. But when, with variations in the circumstances, these goods become instrumental means without which the basic real goods that all human beings need cannot be satisfied, then new derivative natural rights arise. There is no variation in basic natural rights, but only in the derivative natural rights that are rights to the goods which are instrumental in satisfying the human need for basic real goods.

One footnote must be appended to the doctrine of natural needs and natural rights. It cannot be denied that drug addicts and alcoholics have a real need for the poisons to which they have become habituated. Our recognition of the fact that what they really need is not really good for them to have leads us to regard these needs as pathological rather than natural. They exist only in certain individuals under certain circumstances, not in all human beings under all circumstances.

If readers, confronted with the controversy about natural needs and natural rights, should decide against the doctrine I have tried to defend, have they no alternative but to acquiesce in the view that good and evil are entirely subjective as well as in the view that value judgments and prescriptive statements of what ought to be sought or done are neither true nor false?

There is one alternative to which they can repair, but in my judgment it is not a satisfactory alternative, nor one that fully preserves the objectivity of good and evil.

The categorical imperative of Immanuel Kant is thought to provide the criteria for distinguishing between what is right and wrong in human conduct. Whereas the categorical imperative to seek whatever is really good for human beings is based on the needs inherent in human nature, the Kantian categorical imperative to obey the moral law is based on the rational necessity of that law, not upon human nature.

The maxim that we should do unto others what we would have them do unto us (which is just another way of saying that reason requires sound rules of conduct to be capable of universal application) does not tell us what we would have others do unto us. We cannot answer that question in an objective and valid manner without knowing what is really good for us. But, according to Kant, the only thing that is really good in this world is a good will—a will that complies with the moral law, a willingness to do one's duty according to the moral law.

In my judgment, the Kantian position is unsatisfactory (as I have pointed out before) because it gives primacy to the right over the good. It does this by replacing discoverable natural desires by rationally formulated duties as the source of the moral law and the categorical imperative. This leads to the view that the only thing that is really good is a good will, and this, in my judgment, is a grievously inadequate rendering of the idea of goodness.

It has been said that there is no accounting for tastes. Whether this is true or not is the most important question that confronts us in our thinking about the idea of beauty.

It would appear to be true with regard to individual preferences in the sphere of purely sensual pleasures. The differences in individual taste with regard to foods, wines, climates, or sexual partners may not be accountable. If we had perfect knowledge of individual temperaments and of all the factors that have influenced the development of individuals from birth onward, their differences in taste might be explained. The unaccountability of differences in taste arises from the fact that such knowledge is not available, nor is it ever likely to be.

When we pass from variations in taste with regard to purely sensual pleasures to variations in taste with regard to enjoyable beauty, the question of accountability may require a different answer. Here we have grounds for thinking that experts in a given field of objects are better judges of the admirable beauty of those objects than individuals who have neither the knowledge nor the skill requisite for making an expert judgment.

The experts may not always agree about the gradations of admirable beauty exhibited by the objects before them. They may differ in judging which is more beautiful than another and which is the most beautiful of all. But they are likely to agree in their judgments about which objects are admirable for the beauty that lies in their intrinsic excellence and which should be put aside as devoid of admirable beauty in any degree.

If, in the judgment of experts in a certain field of objects, some objects have admirable beauty and others lack it, why does not everyone find enjoyable beauty in the objects thus selected? The fact seems to be that a vast number of persons are likely to find enjoyable beauty in objects dismissed by the experts as devoid of admirable beauty. Similarly, when the experts do agree about one object having more admirable beauty than another, it does not follow that everyone will find more enjoyable beauty in that object. On the contrary, many will find more enjoyable beauty in less admirable objects.

To say that there is no accounting for such differences in taste is to concede that the disconnection between admirable and enjoyable beauty and the absence of any correlation between what experts judge to be more admirable and what others find to be more enjoyable cannot be overcome. If we could account for such differences in taste (which is to say, if we knew their causes), we might be able to find a remedy for them and, by applying it, remove them.

The existence of experts with regard to both admirable and enjoyable beauty in a certain field of objects may provide us with a clue to the solution of this problem. To call certain individuals expert judges of such matters is to attribute superior taste to them. Their having superior taste consists in their finding enjoyable beauty in objects that are admirable for their intrinsic excellence and, with regard to such objects, in enjoying more the beauty of objects that are more admirable.

What is the source of such superior taste? How did the experts come to possess it? The answer is to be found in the factors that, in the course of their personal development, made them expert judges with regard to a certain field of objects. These factors include their abundant exposure to the objects in question, their patient, attentive, and sustained experience of them, their knowledge about the elements that enter into the production of such objects, and even perhaps their possession of some degree of skill in producing them.

If I am correct in this account of what makes certain individuals expert judges with regard to the admirable beauty of objects of a certain kind, then we are also able to account for their superior taste with regard to the enjoyable beauty of the objects in question.

It follows that inferior taste can be accounted for in a parallel manner. It results from the absence, in the development of some individuals, of the very same factors the presence of which confers expert judgment and superior taste on other individuals.

Inferior taste consists in finding enjoyable beauty in objects that are devoid of admirable beauty or in finding more enjoyable beauty in objects that are less admirable. Our being able to account for it should also enable us to remedy it. The remedy lies in the cultivation of taste by the operation of the very same factors that explain the possession of expert judgment and superior taste.

Knowing the remedy is one thing. Being able to apply it effectively and universally is another.

We know, for example, that the morally virtuous person is one who takes pleasure in acquiring real goods and in making the right choices. But we also know that it is extremely difficult, if not impossible, to so rear the young of the human race that all turn out to be morally virtuous men and women.

We are left in the same plight by knowing that the aesthetically virtuous or the aesthetically cultivated person is one who finds enjoyable beauty in objects that are admirable for the beauty of their intrinsic excellence. We may have to acknowledge that it remains extremely difficult, if not impossible, to so cultivate the taste of human beings in the course of their personal development that all or even a fairly sizable number of them come to acquire the superior taste possessed by experts with regard to a certain field of objects.

Readers must, therefore, be left with questions they will have to answer for themselves. Can taste with regard to beauty be accounted for? Can good taste be cultivated and bad taste be cured? To what extent can these desirable objectives be accomplished?

Only if the answers tend to be affirmative and optimistic is there any basis for concluding that what is generally admirable in the sphere of beauty should also be generally enjoyable, and the more admirable the object the more enjoyable it should be.

CHAPTER 28

Concerning Liberty, Equality, and Justice

THE CENTRAL ISSUES and most important questions concerning truth, goodness, and beauty bear on the objectivity of these three fundamental values. The picture is quite different in the case of liberty, equality, and justice.

In dealing with these ideas, we have seen that each is conceived in a number of different ways. We have considered the diverse modes of freedom, the several dimensions of equality, the different aspects of justice. The issues that come to the forefront here involve disputes about whether one or another conception of freedom, equality, and justice is the only correct conception of it, whether one takes precedence over the others, or whether the soundest and most adequate theory of the matter is one that embraces all of the various conceptions in an orderly and significant way.

In the sphere of liberty, only one of the three major forms of freedom has never been denied reality. That is liberty of action in society—the circumstantial freedom of the individual to do as he pleases without let or hindrance, so long as the exercise of such liberty does not turn into license by violating laws that prohibit doing injury to others or to the community as a whole.

Even among those who avoid the libertarian error of asking for unlimited freedom of action, with no distinction between liberty and license, there is difference of opinion concerning the relation of liberty to law—the natural moral law or the positive law of a civil society.

Some, like John Stuart Mill, hold that individuals are free only in that area of human conduct not regulated by law, so that as the sphere of law enlarges, the sphere of liberty contracts.

Others, like John Locke, hold on the contrary that individuals are not only free "where the law prescribes not," but also when they act in obedience to laws that are constitutionally enacted by a government to which they have given their consent. Being politically free citizens of a republic, with a voice in their own government, they are also free when they obey laws in the making of which they have directly or indirectly participated.

In taking this position, John Locke affirms still another kind of freedom—the freedom that the virtuous man possesses in being able to will as he ought, in being able to conform his will to the moral or the civil law that prescribes just conduct and prohibits injustice.

Only those who recognize that virtuous persons stand in a special relation to law, quite different from the posture of vicious or criminal individuals, can understand why obedience to just laws justly made in no way infringes upon freedom of action. That special relation consists in their having the freedom to will as they ought.

Vicious or criminal individuals, lacking such freedom, regard the coercive force of law as greatly curtailing their freedom to do as they please. They do not respond to the law's authority, but only to its coercive force; and, being constrained by it, they feel unfree.

This reveals a significant difference between the view of freedom held by those who affirm only the circumstantial freedom to do as one pleases and those who affirm liberty of action as subordinate to the liberty that is acquired with virtue—the freedom to will as one ought.

It is possible to go too far in stressing the importance of the latter freedom. To regard it as the only freedom worth having and thereby to dismiss liberty of action as having little or no value in human life is to obliterate the distinction between the free man and the slave, or worse, to think that even a slave in chains can achieve happiness because he has the only thing requisite for it—a good or virtuous will and the moral liberty that goes with it.

The most intensely disputed issue concerning freedom is, as everyone knows, the age-old controversy about man's inherent possession of a free will and, with it, freedom of choice.

The determinists, who deny such freedom on the grounds that it is incompatible with the causal laws that govern the physical world of which man is a part, can affirm only one of the three major forms of freedom—liberty of action in society, freedom from coercion or constraint.

They must perforce deny the acquired freedom to will as one ought, for moral liberty presupposes freedom of choice. Denying moral liberty, which involves voluntary compliance with the dictates of the moral and civil law, they must also be uneasy with, or reject, the distinction between liberty and license and think that individuals are free only when their conduct is unconstrained by the coercive force of law.

Those who affirm the one freedom that is conceived as being inherent in human nature do so on the following grounds. Though they regard man as a part of nature, they also think he is so *only in part*.

In their view, the action of the human intellect and will may be conditioned by the action of the brain as a physical mechanism, but it is not wholly governed by the physical—or bio-physical and biochemical—laws that govern the brain and other of man's physical organs.

To affirm the freedom of the will one need not go to the extreme of attributing to man a spirituality that totally tran-scends physical nature and so is entirely exempt from the reign of its causal laws. One need only maintain that the physical basis of human behavior constitutes a necessary, but not a suf-ficient, condition for the action of the human mind in either thinking or willing.

Accordingly, exponents of the view that man inherently pos-sesses freedom of choice reject the argument of the determinists that such freedom violates the laws of physical nature. The underlying issue between them is generated by their conflict-ing views concerning human nature—as not radically different from the nature of other physical organisms or as transcending the physical world, at least in part.

I pointed out earlier that moral liberty presupposes freedom of choice. I must now repeat another point made earlier; namely, that the natural right to liberty of action also presup-poses freedom of choice. It is based on the need for liberty of action as a means to be employed in the pursuit of happiness.

We cannot be charged with the moral responsibility for mak-ing good human lives for ourselves if we are not free to execute our choices in actions that are not constrained by any impedi-ment except those imposed by just laws. Without free choice, we cannot be free to will as we ought. Without free choice and moral liberty, we are not entitled to the freedom of acting as we wish in accordance with a willingness to act as we ought.

If I am right in the foregoing account of opposing views with regard to liberty—and this readers must decide for themselves—then the soundest and most adequate theory of freedom is one that affirms all three of the major freedoms: natural freedom of choice, acquired moral liberty, and circumstantial freedom of action, the last of these conjoined with the political liberty of enfranchised citizens under constitutional government.

The most fundamental issue with regard to equality pivots on the affirmation or denial of the proposition that all human beings are equal in their common humanity and *only* in that respect.

As persons, they are all equally human. None is more or less human than another, though they may be unequal, one with another, in the degree to which they possess the species-specific properties that are present in all members of the human species.

This view of the personal equality of all human beings is denied by those who divide mankind, as Aristotle did, into persons who are at birth endowed with the capacity to live as free individuals, able to direct the conduct of their lives, and those who are at birth deficient, lacking in their makeup the capacity for self-direction.

The inequality thus thought to exist between two portions of mankind is not regarded as a difference in the degree to which individuals possess the same native endowments. Rather it involves a difference in kind between two groups—the one having native endowments lacked by the other.

The distinction here introduced between equality or inequality in kind and equality or inequality in degree has far-reaching consequences. A massive array of undeniable facts prevents us from asserting that all human beings are not only equal in kind, but also equal in the degree to which they possess the properties inherent in their common human nature.

If we reject the Aristotelian view or views similar to it, which divide the human race into two unequal kinds of human beings, we cannot reject the view that all human beings, equal in kind, are nevertheless individually unequal in degree in many significant respects. Two individuals may, of course, be equal in the degree in which they possess some human attributes, but it is seldom if ever the case that two individuals are equal in the degree to which they possess all human attributes.

Upon the affirmation that all human beings are personally equal in their humanity rests the acknowledgment that all are

entitled to a circumstantial equality of conditions and a circumstantial equality of opportunity. From the acknowledgment that
individuals, equal in kind, are also unequal in degree in many
diverse respects—not only in their native endowments but also
in their acquired attainments and how they put both to use in
the actions they perform or the services they render—follows
the further consequence that justice requires inequalities in the
degree to which individuals receive rewards for what they do.

Egalitarians, who, with regard to the circumstantial equality
of conditions, advocate the elimination of all inequalities in
degree, fail to recognize that the personal equality of human
beings in kind together with their personal inequality in degree
leads to two conclusions, not one.

It is not enough to conclude that all human beings deserve an
equality of treatment or of conditions that is an equality in
kind. It is also necessary to conclude that individuals, unequal
in degree in respects that are significant, deserve an inequality
of treatment or of conditions that is an inequality in degree.

The fundamental distinction between equality or inequality
in kind and equality or inequality in degree is challenged by
those who think that the only equality and inequality is an
equality or inequality in degree. They reject the notion of
equality and inequality in kind on the ground that it departs
from the conception of inequality as consisting in one thing
being more and another less in a certain respect and from the
conception of equality as consisting in one thing being neither
more nor less than another in a certain respect.

Being more or less is a difference in degree. Being neither
more nor less is the absence of any difference in degree. Hence
inequality, rightly conceived, must always involve a difference
in degree; and equality, rightly conceived, must always consist
in no difference in degree.

If the notion of equality were thus restricted, we could not
affirm that human beings are all equally human in kind while
being, at the same time, individually unequal in degree, one
with another, in any number of significant respects. It would

also be impossible to affirm the opposite view—that mankind is divided into two unequal groups of human beings, differing in kind, not just in degree, because one group possesses certain native endowments totally lacked by the other, not just possessed by the other group to a lesser degree.

Nevertheless, it is necessary to meet the challenge of the egalitarian by showing that the notion of equality and inequality in kind conforms to the conception of equality as consisting in two things being neither more nor less, and of inequality as consisting in one thing being more than the other in a certain respect.

Two concrete examples will be helpful in doing what is required. Let us first consider political equality and inequality, then economic equality and inequality.

Political equality in kind exists in any society in which all individuals entitled by their political nature to political liberty are granted the status of citizenship with suffrage. Political inequality in kind exists in any society in which some individuals are enfranchised and some are disfranchised and are thus deprived of political liberty and political participation through suffrage. In the latter case, one group of individuals *has* what the other group totally *lacks*. This is not a difference in degree, but a difference in kind.

When the population is divided into two groups, one of which has political status, powers, rights, and privileges lacked by the other, the members of the have group enjoy either enough or more than enough of the conditions to which all human beings are entitled. The have-not group, deprived of these conditions, have less than enough if they are subjects ruled without their own consent or without a voice in government but nevertheless ruled for their own good, or they may have nothing at all if they are chattel slaves used as instruments of production.

The inequality in kind between the political haves and have-nots can thus be seen as an inequality that involves a distinction between more and less. The haves have enough political power, or more than enough when they are citizens occupying political office and exercising the powers vested in such offices. The have-nots have less than enough political power or none at all.

The line that divides enough or more than enough from less than enough or none at all appeals to a standard of *enoughness* that is measured by the amount to which all human beings are entitled by virtue of their natural rights.

Economic equality and inequality in kind presents the same picture. All human beings are entitled to a certain amount of wealth, in the form of various economic goods, as a condition they need to lead decent human lives. That measure of wealth, however it is determined, is enough. Some individuals, having enough for the pursuit of happiness, may also deserve to acquire more than enough by the contribution they make to the production of wealth. Those who do not have the measure of wealth to which all human beings are entitled by natural right have less than enough in varying degrees of deprivation, down to the state of destitution that carries with it the threat of starvation and death.

A society in which all individuals or families have either enough or more than enough wealth is one in which there exists an economic equality in kind, accompanied by inequalities in degree. A society in which some individuals or families are economic haves and some are economic have-nots is one in which an inequality in kind exists, accompanied by inequalities in degrees both above and below the line that divides those who have enough or more than enough from those who do not have enough and are deprived in varying degrees.

Let us for the moment consider equality and inequality in kind apart from the possibility of its being accompanied, as it usually is and should be, by inequalities in degree. Then we can make the point under consideration crystal clear. Two individuals equal in kind, politically or economically, have neither more nor less than enough of the political conditions to which all human beings are entitled. Of two individuals who are unequal in kind, politically or economically, one enjoys the requisite conditions in a measure that is enough and the other is deprived of them in a measure that is less than enough.

In my judgment, a sound and adequate theory of equality is one that includes all the dimensions of equality—personal and circumstantial equality and inequality, equality and inequality in kind as well as equality and inequality in degree.

In the sphere of circumstantial equality, it must also include equality of opportunity as well as equality of treatment, conditions, and results. In doing so, it should subordinate equality of opportunity to equality of conditions and results.

To insist that equality of opportunity is the only circumstantial equality to which individuals are entitled is to deny that all persons are entitled by right to an equality of conditions that makes them all equal in kind as political and economic haves.

I have indicated the differences of opinion that separate exponents of different theories of equality on major issues about that idea. I have also indicated where I stand on these issues. Whether the views I have advanced are the correct ones, readers must decide for themselves.

With regard to the idea of justice, the central and predominant controversy consists in a three-sided dispute. There are three conflicting theories, two ancient, one modern.

Coming down to us from antiquity is the view that might makes right. This, in the course of centuries, became the legalist or positivist theory of justice, which holds that, antecedent to the positive law of the state that carries with it the force of the sovereign, nothing is either just or unjust. Unjust acts are those prohibited by the positive law; just acts those prescribed by it.

Equally ancient is the view that natural justice is antecedent to legal justice—that the precepts of the natural moral law and the existence of natural rights determine what is just and unjust prior to and independent of legislative enactments by *de facto* or *de jure* governments. This being the case, states, constitutions, governments, and their laws can be judged just or unjust by reference to natural rights and the principles of natural justice.

The third side in this three-cornered dispute is the utilitarian or pragmatic theory of justice, which emerged in the nineteenth century. According to this view, the criteria of what is just or unjust in human actions as well as in the acts or policies of governments and in the laws they make and enforce derive from the consideration of the ultimate end to be served—called the "general happiness" or "the greatest good for the greatest number" by the early utilitarians, but equally well named when it is called "the general welfare" or "the common good." Acts, policies, and laws are just to the extent that they serve and promote the general welfare or the common good; unjust to the extent that they injure it or detract from it.

In my view of the matter, each of these three theories of justice is false when it claims to be the whole truth, excluding what is sound in the other two theories. Though I favor the naturalist theory as sounder than either of the other two, I must concede that when it claims to be able to answer all questions about justice by reference to natural rights, it goes too far. The questions it can answer are of prime importance, but they fall short of being all the questions that call for answers.

Similarly, the claim that all questions of justice can be answered by reference to criteria of fairness in exchanges or distributions is excessive. Some, but only some, certainly can be, and these are of secondary importance.

Questions about justice that cannot be answered by reference to natural rights or criteria of fairness can be answered by the consideration of what is expedient or inexpedient in relation to the general welfare or the common good. However, many— though not all—determinations of what serves or disserves the general welfare or the common good turn out upon examination to be identical with determinations of the just and the unjust by reference to natural rights or to criteria of fairness. The protection of natural rights from violation and the requirement of fairness in exchanges and distributions are highly expedient social policies. They promote the general welfare or the common good.

Finally, the claim made by the legalists or positivists that all questions of justice can be answered by reference to laws enacted by the state and enforced by a government in power can be embraced only by those who are unashamed to espouse the extreme doctrine that might makes right. Nevertheless, a retreat from that extreme must admit that some determinations of what is just or unjust stem solely from the enactment of ordinances that decide which of several alternative policies should be adopted as expedient in the service of the public interest.

None of these alternatives is to be recommended on the ground that it secures natural rights or that it represents fair dealing. None is superior to the others as being more expedient in the service of the general welfare. Therefore, it is only the enactment of a positive law embodying that alternative which determines what is just in this case.

The reconciliation of the three conflicting theories of justice can be accomplished by avoiding the excessive claim each makes and by putting what is true in each of them together in a well-ordered manner. This can be briefly set forth as follows.

Everything that is just by reference to natural rights or just by reference to criteria of fairness is also just through being expedient in the service of the common good or general welfare. What is just by reference to natural rights takes priority over what is just by reference to criteria of fairness because the latter is based on the personal equalities and inequalities of individuals—their endowments and attainments and how they put them to use—whereas the former is based on the natural needs common to all persons as members of the human race.

Everything that is expedient in the service of the common good or general welfare is just because it serves that end, but it may not always be just also by reference to natural rights or to criteria of fairness. Herein lies the special truth contributed by the pragmatic or utilitarian theory of justice.

All of the foregoing determinations of what is just or unjust can be made antecedent to the enactment of positive laws by the state. In fact, the enactment of positive laws that are just embodies the foregoing determinations of what is just.

However, some things cannot be thus determined to be either just or unjust. They are morally indifferent in the sense that they are neither for nor against natural rights, neither fair nor unfair, neither more nor less expedient in the public interest.

Nevertheless, in the public interest, one or another alternative course of action must be decided upon. When this decision is made by legislative enactment, a course of action prescribed by positive law becomes just, and one prohibited by positive law becomes unjust. Herein lies the special truth contributed by the legalist or positivist theory of justice.

If the formulation I have just presented is correct (which readers must decide for themselves), the reconciliation of the three conflicting theories has been accomplished by rejecting the extravagant claims made by each of them and by recognizing that each makes an indispensable contribution to the whole truth that is not made by the others. It is also necessary to put these partial contributions together in a way that recognizes the inherent priority of the naturalist theory over the pragmatic or utilitarian theory, and of both over the legalist or positivist theory. When this is done, we end up with a sound and adequate rendering of the idea of justice, and one that, in my judgment, cannot be achieved in any other way.

We are still left with the two most difficult questions about justice that have ever been raised. Both were raised by Plato at the very beginning of our Western thinking about justice. One, I think, can be answered; but the other may be unanswerable.

The first of these two questions is, Why should anyone be just in his or her action toward others or in relation to the community in which he or she lives?

This question was raised by Plato in the first two books of his *Republic*, in the context of inquiring whether the individual who acts justly profits from it in terms of his own happiness. In other words, should the individual act justly because it is expedient for him to do so on the grounds that his justice toward others promotes the pursuit of his own happiness?

On the face of it, the answer would appear to be negative. Even the acknowledgment that being virtuous is expedient as a means to happiness does not lead to a positive answer.

To make what is ultimately a whole good life, the individual must, of course, make the right choices concerning the goods he needs and wants. Moral virtue is the firm habit that disposes the individual to make such choices.

The habitually intemperate individual, who wrongly chooses to indulge in excessive desires for merely apparent goods that afford immediate pleasure, in preference to the real goods he or she in the long run needs, moves in a direction that departs from the route to his or her ultimate good. The same thing can be said of the habitual coward, who, lacking fortitude, turns away from the real goods he should seek because of the pains to be endured or the difficulties to be overcome in acquiring them.

So far it is clear that being morally virtuous (at least to the extent of being temperate and courageous) is not only worthy in itself but also expedient as an indispensable means to achieving a good human life. But what about that aspect of moral virtue that is called justice?

As I see it, the only answer must lie in a truth that is difficult to explain and that is seldom understood. If the moral virtues I have named—temperance, courage, and justice—were three separate habits any one of which a person might possess without having the others, then I, for one, would not know how to argue for the expediency of being just toward others as a means to my own happiness. However, if, on the contrary, the three habits named are distinct but not separable aspects of moral virtue as an integral and indivisible whole, then the answer sought is in sight.

The argument runs as follows. I cannot achieve the happiness of a good human life without being morally virtuous—without having the firm habit of making right choices. I cannot be morally virtuous in one respect without being morally virtuous in all respects, because the three aspects of moral virtue that I have named are inseparable from one another.

I cannot be temperate without being courageous and just. I cannot be courageous without being temperate and just. If I am unjust, I cannot be either temperate or courageous. But intemperance on my part and lack of fortitude will defeat my pursuit of happiness. Hence injustice on my part will defeat it also.

Therefore, in order to succeed in my effort to achieve my own ultimate good, which is a good human life as a whole, I must be just in my actions toward others and in relation to the community in which I live.

What underlies this argument and explains the truth on which it rests is a fundamental insight into the nature of moral virtue as a direction of human conduct toward the ultimate and common good. Our actions are directed either toward that end or away from it.

A given choice or act cannot be pointed in both directions at once. Nor can we have the habit of moving in that direction when we make choices with respect to our own good, while at the same time having the habit of moving in the opposite direction when we make choices with respect to the good of others.

Moral virtue being one integral whole, with a diversity of distinct but inseparable aspects, it always points us in one and the same direction whether we are considering our own happiness or the happiness of others. That is why my being just to others is also expedient as a means toward the attainment of my own happiness.

The other question Plato asked was, Is it better to suffer injustice at the hands of others or to be unjust toward them? The question presupposes, of course, that we are confronted with this difficult choice: We must either act unjustly toward others or suffer unjust treatment by them. Faced with these alternatives, which should we choose?

Plato himself was persuaded that the choice should always be to suffer injustice rather than do it. In his view, no injury that we can suffer at the hands of others can possibly be as destructive of our well-being as taking unto ourselves the moral evil of being unjust toward others. That view rests on an inadequate understanding of human happiness or well-being.

Toward the end of the trial of Socrates, Plato has him say that no harm can come to a good man in this life or the next. If this is interpreted to mean that the morally good or virtuous man cannot be seriously harmed by any external injury inflicted upon him by others; if, in other words, the only serious injury that an individual can suffer is one he inflicts upon himself by conduct that is not morally right or virtuous, then we can see why Plato thought that it is always much better to suffer injustice than to do it.

My rejection of Plato's view of the matter turns on a conception of human happiness that involves the possession of all the things that are really good for a person, among which a morally good or virtuous will is *only one*, however important that one may be. Life and liberty, knowledge and friends, health and a modicum of wealth and other goods of fortune—all these are also real goods the possession of which is indispensable to a good human life.

This being so, my pursuit of happiness can be seriously impaired or even defeated by the injuries I suffer if I am enslaved, if my health is maimed, if I am deprived of sufficient wealth, if I am kept in ignorance, and so on. These are injuries I can suffer at the hands of others or from the injustice of the society in which I live.

I, therefore, think that there is no general answer to Plato's question about doing and suffering injustice. In particular cases, it may be possible to decide that, confronted with certain alternatives, it is better to suffer injustice than to do it, because the injury suffered results only in a slight impediment to my pursuit of happiness, whereas the injury I inflict upon myself by being unjust may have much more serious consequences for my moral character. However, the latter would be the case only if my act of injustice in this one instance should lead to subsequent similar acts that then altered my habitual disposition and ended up in my loss of moral virtue itself, which is very unlikely.

The choice between doing and suffering injustice becomes a difficult and onerous one only when the external injury that threatens us would result in a total deprivation of one or another real good that we need in order to live well. If, in order to avoid the serious injury that threatens our happiness, we have to commit one act of injustice and one that does not lead to the loss of moral virtue on our part (because one act neither makes nor breaks a habit), then it may be clearly preferable to do injustice in this one instance rather than to suffer it.